HOW Y'ALL DOING?

Also by Leslie Jordan

My Trip Down the Pink Carpet

HOW Y'ALL DOING? Copyright © 2021 by Leslie Jordan. Introduction
and photo insert © 2022 by Leslie Jordan. All rights reserved. Printed
in the United States of America. No part of this book may be used or
reproduced in any manner whatsoever without written permission
except in the case of brief quotations embodied in critical articles
and reviews. For information, address HarperCollins Publishers, 195
Broadway, New York, NY 10007.

HarperCollins books may be purchased for educational, business,
or sales promotional use. For information, please email the Special
Markets Department at SPsales@harpercollins.com.

A hardcover edition of this book was published in 2021 by
William Morrow, an imprint of HarperCollins Publishers.

FIRST WILLIAM MORROW PAPERBACK EDITION PUBLISHED 2022.

Designed by Bonni Leon-Berman

Library of Congress Cataloging-in-Publication Data
has been applied for.

ISBN 978-0-06-307620-4

23 24 25 26 27 LBC 8 7 6 5 4

Leslie Jordan

HOW Y'ALL DOING?

Misadventures and Mischief from a Life Well Lived

WILLIAM MORROW
An Imprint of HarperCollins*Publishers*

CONTENTS

My dear friend and fellow reader,

You hold in your hot little hands the paperback edition of my book *How Y'all Doing? Misadventures and Mischief from a Life Well Lived.* It gives me immense pleasure that you are about to read my book and I hope you enjoy it. I am doubly pleased that you have chosen the paperback edition.

I have a long and varied history with paperback books. Call me crazy, but I love paperbacks twice as much as the hardback editions. I suppose I found that paperbacks have always taken a back seat to hardback editions. That's unfair! I remember for years and years, I only displayed my hardback editions. They sat there on the shelf, proudly gleaming with their own self-worth. I'm sure that made my paperbacks felt ashamed. I didn't mean any harm. It just seemed like the way it should be. Hardback editions cost more and are always trotted out months and sometimes years before the paperbacks are allowed to even see the light of day.

But most people, if they are like me, could not afford the hardback edition. Unless you could find the book at the local library, you had to wait for the paperback to come out. Because of that, I only have a small number of hardbacks compared to the thousands of paperbacks I own. I have kept every paperback I ever bought. That cannot be said of those hardback editions. In my younger years, I moved all over the place. I went from one end of this country to another. Hardbacks I lost or left behind along the way, but paperbacks taped in boxes always seem to end up wherever I was. They would be under the bed or stacked in a garage. But now I proudly display my paperbacks next to my hardbacks because I love them both equally!

So, my dear friend and fellow reader, have at it! Carry this paperback in your back pocket, in your purse, or your knapsack; wherever it is that you put your stuff as you move around on your daily routine. Pull it out at the bus stop, on the airplane, under a tree at lunchtime, while you're snuggled in your bed before sleep, anywhere you want. The more dog-eared it becomes, the better, I say.

Just please read and enjoy.

And when you are through; when you've reached the last page, display it proudly amongst your hardbacks.

I know this little dog-eared paperback of *How Y'all Doing?* will feel right at home.

Love Light Leslie

HOW Y'ALL DOING?

HOW Y'ALL DOING?

"Well, shit. How y'all doing?"

That's how all this started.

When I was growing up, I was not allowed to cuss. It was just not the way I was raised. So, I don't cuss. At least, I don't cuss too much. My mother was none too happy I garnered such success using the word "shit," but that's how it all happened—how, in ten easy steps, I became an Instagram maven.

I had to look up the word "maven" to make sure I am using it right. I am not. When I was looking it up, I also learned that Maven is a girl's name in Hebrew, but it can also be used as a boy's name. It translates as "one who understands."

Well, I certainly do NOT understand Instagram. I'm

a complete neophyte. But somehow, as so often happens in this crazy world, I amassed a gobsmacking number of followers. Five and a half million at last count. I think I need to say that again, because sometimes I cannot comprehend the magnitude.

I have five and a half million friends on Instagram!

I may not be the only person on Instagram to achieve that many followers in such a short time, to go from zero to well over five million in about six months, but here's the deal: I would imagine most people on Instagram with millions of followers were already a known commodity when they started their Instagram account.

Yes, I was on TV and in movies, but it seems that most of my followers say they "discovered" me on Instagram.

That seems to be what this newfound success is all about. Whether they thought they knew me from my parts on television, my parts in the movies or my stage parts, through the magic of Instagram, they got to know the real Leslie Allen Jordan.

Here's how my road to Instagram fame began.

I was working on a short-lived but wonderful series on Fox TV called *The Cool Kids*. The show had originally been presented to me as a pilot from "the boys" in a very popular TV show called *It's Always Sunny in Philadelphia,* a funny sitcom about friends in a fictional bar in

Philadelphia who are always willing to turn on each other for profit or personal gain.

I thought it was so irreverent and unlike anything else on TV. Plus the three male stars, Glenn Howerton, Rob McElhenney and Charlie Day, were really cute.

Anything these boys came up with, count me in!

On *The Cool Kids*, my character's name was Sid and had originally been written as a seventy-year-old straight Jewish man from Brooklyn. I drove to the audition (and, yes, I had to audition) befuddled. I could not understand why they would even be interested in my playing the part. I can play a lot of things, but I did not think I could pull off a seventy-year-old straight Jewish man from Brooklyn.

Oy vey.

So, I winged it. I threw caution to the wind, walked in the door and announced to all those present in the audition room that I was going to "put a different spin on things."

I launched into my usual schtick. I made the character younger, Southern and gay. I did everything but tap-dance with sparklers and turn cartwheels. I was my usual shameless self.

I got the job.

I found out later that the road to being hired on this new series had actually begun on the set of *Will &*

Grace. I had won an Emmy Award back in 2006 for my portrayal of Beverley Leslie. When the show was re-booted for three brand-new seasons, I was so excited to be playing Beverley again. On one episode, I worked with the actor Max Greenfield, of *New Girl* fame. We really hit it off and giggled the whole time like two little school-girls.

Max is the gayest straight man I know. I mean this as the highest compliment possible. He embodies the best of both worlds and is a spectacular human being.

And I adore him.

He is married to Tess Sanchez, who used to be the head of casting for Fox TV. When Tess told Max about this new series she was casting, he brought my name up. They both told their friend Charlie Day that he should at least audition me for the seventy-year-old straight Jewish man from Brooklyn. Just in case they might want to go another way with the character.

Years ago, I had been told by Barbara Miller, the legendary casting director, that when I died, on my tombstone, it should read, HERE LIES THE OTHER WAY TO GO.

She liked to bring me in to audition for producers even though I might not have been right for a particular part. She would introduce me as perhaps "the other way to go" with the character.

HOW Y'ALL DOING?

Sometimes it would blow up right in front of us, as the producers would just sit there and stare stonily as I auditioned, the looks on their faces saying it all.

"What is he doing here, Barbara? He's not what we are looking for at all."

But then, sometimes, it was magical. The producers would lean forward as I auditioned. And once again, the looks on their faces would say it all.

"Wow. We did not think of the character in this manner, but this is interesting."

And I would book the job.

But the story of how I became an internet success has an even more winding road.

When I was young, there were three female comedians whom I adored: Lily Tomlin, Phyllis Diller and Carol Burnett.

I could impersonate all three perfectly. I knew all their routines! I would jump up and do them at the drop of a hat. That must have been quite a sight. A twelve-year-old boy impersonating female comedians.

But I was born to perform.

Over the years, I honed all those impersonation skills into a lifetime of performing my one-man show all over the globe.

Sometimes I was performing in up to forty-four venues a year.

One night, at a performance of my show in Los Angeles, I looked out and Phyllis Diller was in the front row. Phyllis Diller was there to see me! I was so overjoyed; I called my mother from backstage to tell her Miss Diller was in the audience.

"Mom, remember when I was little and I could act out Phyllis Diller's routines? She's here! In my audience in the front row!"

After the performance, I walked out into the theater's audience and there sat Miss Diller, all alone, waiting for me. I could tell she had been crying, as one of her famous false eyelashes had come unglued. It flapped precariously above her eye and gave her a slightly crazed look.

But there were other things on her mind, things she wanted to tell me.

"Young man," she gushed, "that was a wonderful show. Your speech at the end really got to me, as I have tried to express the same sentiment to my children their whole life."

At that time, I used to end my show by saying, "Happiness is a choice. Happiness is a habit. And happiness is something you have to work hard at. It does not just happen."

What a sweet, dear lady Phyllis Diller was. And tiny. Teeny tiny, like me. She was so deserving of my heroine worship.

I then got to meet Lily Tomlin in 2007, on a series we did called *12 Miles of Bad Road*. When we first met, I glommed on and would not let go. When we were shooting our first scene together and having such a good time, Linda Bloodworth-Thomason, who wrote the series, remarked, "Good Lord, the two of you are like a couple of vaudeville comedians!"

When it comes to getting the laugh, Lily Tomlin is as shameless as me.

She and I have remained fast friends for years now. Forget that she is a brilliant comedienne. Even more important, she is a sterling human being. She, along with her longtime partner and now wife, Jane Wagner, jumped in and helped take my one-man show to New York. Imagine, having Lily Tomlin and Jane Wagner as producers on the marquee at your Off-Broadway debut.

It was the thrill of a lifetime.

Lily even pulled some strings and got us both on *The View* to promote the show. I got so nervous, I walked out, took one look at Whoopi and Joy Behar and started running my mouth. All of a sudden, one of them said we had to wrap it up and I realized I had not let Lily say a word. I was on a major talk show with a legendary comedienne and I had just silenced a legend.

Not one single word.

When we walked off the set with the cameras following us, Lily chased me down the hall, pretending to berate me for being so selfish as to not let her get a word in edgewise.

Good thing I can run faster than Lily Tomlin.

Of my youthful heroine triumvirate, the only comedienne I am sad to say I have not yet met is Miss Carol Burnett. But on *The Cool Kids*, I was lucky enough to work with her partner in comedy Vicki Lawrence.

I have always loved the story of how Carol Burnett discovered Vicki. When Vicki was seventeen years old, she competed in a "firefighter's beauty contest."

Whatever the hell that is!

The winner was to be crowned "Miss Fireball." This was all happening in Miss Lawrence's hometown of Inglewood, California, in 1967. The local paper wrote a story about how much Vicki Lawrence looked like Carol Burnett. Vicki, being the plucky woman she is, cut the article out, sealed it in a letter, and sent it to Miss Burnett.

HOW Y'ALL DOING?

Within a few months, Vicki Lawrence was playing Carol Burnett's sister on *The Carol Burnett Show*!

As a kid, I would lie on my stomach in front of the tube, shrieking hysterically at their shenanigans, week after week.

When I found out that Vicki had signed on to do *The Cool Kids*, I was beside myself. I was one degree closer to my last great comedy heroine. Vicki Lawrence is exactly like you think she would be. What you see is what you get, and what you get is a wonderfully loving, exceptionally talented lady.

Also cast in *The Cool Kids* was David Alan Grier. I had been a fan of his since the days of *In Living Color* in the early 1990s. When he came out on-screen in the "Men on Film" sketch and "double snapped" his fingers as Antoine Merriweather, I fell out! I thought it was the funniest thing I had ever seen on TV. The sketch was about two gay cultural critics commenting on all kinds of things, from movies to art to television. With Damon Wayans playing Blaine Edwards, his equally sissy cohort, they took the country by storm.

There were a lot of gay people who thought this extremely effeminate performance was offensive and portrayed gay men in a bad light. Especially since all this nonsense was coming from two straight men.

Not me!

I hollered.

Honey, we gotta be able to laugh at ourselves. What a lot of people do not know is that David was in the cast of *Dreamgirls* on Broadway in 1981. The character he created for the sketch was based on all the gay men he'd worked with in the theater world. This was the way they talked! This was their world. He was privy to it all backstage during the musical's long run.

His performance came from a very loving place, and for me, that was all that mattered!

Rounding out the cast of *The Cool Kids* was dear Martin Mull. What a champion and a delight he was to work with. He once paid me the biggest compliment I have ever received as a performer.

He, too, came to see me in my one-man show. Afterward, he pulled me aside. "Leslie, watching you tonight was like watching a master class in comedy performance. You were brilliant."

My gosh. My gosh. My gosh.

And this from a comedian of his stature.

HOW Y'ALL DOING?

At one of the early rehearsals for *The Cool Kids*, Martin remarked, "If the four of us were in any other line of work and had given the years we've all given to the industry, we would get a gold watch. Maybe this series will be our gold watch. Maybe it will take care of us into our old age."

Well, maybe not, Martin, dear.

The series was canceled after just one season.

But it was on the set of this ill-fated series that my internet success really began. As *The Cool Kids* was a new series, there were always folks from the network's publicity department on the set. They were on the lookout for ways to push this new series into the public's view. Every time I would say something funny, one of the publicists would jump on it. "Post that!" I did not want to appear ignorant, but I had no earthly idea what they meant. I thought maybe it had something to do with those yellow Post-it notes.

Then, one summer evening, we were all gathered over in Beverly Hills at a lawn bowling event the publicity department had cooked up. The press people from all the news outlets were interviewing and photographing the cast as we learned how to lawn bowl.

There was a dinner of sorts and then an outdoor screening of our pilot episode. At one point, I was strolling through the crowd with Tess Sanchez, the person who put me up for the role in the first place, when I said something really funny. She said, "You should post that on your Instagram."

All of a sudden, it hit me.

Oh! So, that is what "post it" means! I told Tess that I did not have an Instagram account. She stopped dead still. "Oh, darling, you really have to get Instagram. It's so important for an actor. Especially right now."

I began to wail, "But why? I don't know how! I barely know how to do Facebook. Technology scares the shit out of me. I am an old man, Tess."

"Don't be silly," she told me. "I'll have one of my girls walk you all the way through the process and hold your hand."

And right there, right that instant, at a lawn bowling event in Beverly Hills, I became a member in good standing of INSTAGRAM.

I would make my posts in my dressing room and ramble on about what was going on with *The Cool Kids*.

Within a few days, I had twenty thousand followers. I could not believe it. When I told the kids in the publicity department, one girl said, "Oh, that's nothing. You'll get more."

I was a tiny bit incensed. I thought twenty thousand was quite a lot. Twenty thousand people checking my Instagram daily to see what I had to post. It was impressive to me.

Then my friend and cohort on *Will & Grace*, Megan Mullally, reposted something funny I had said. I woke up the next day to over eighty thousand followers!

Even though the kids in the publicity department were still not impressed, I thought it was quite an accomplishment.

I stayed at eighty thousand followers for a rather long time. And then the COVID-19 pandemic hit.

During March and April of 2020, I was in Tennessee with my family, as I thought that was a better place to hunker down while the shelter-in-place order was in effect. I rented a lovely but tiny apartment near my family for the duration. I ended up staying almost two months.

Stuck in a tiny apartment by myself for most of the day, every day, it did not take long for boredom to set in. At one point, I thought I was going to go crazy. At least I was able to get out of that small apartment once daily to go over and check on my family.

To pass the time, I started thinking of fun things to post on my Instagram page. Silly stories about my family, baton twirling with a back scratcher, doing yoga stretches up on the kitchen counter, cutting my own hair to old hippie rock music. I was doing just about anything I could come up with.

Right in the midst of all this, my phone rang. It was a friend who was out in California. He told me, "Leslie, you've gone viral."

I quickly answered, "Oh no, honey. I'm fine. I'm staying at my mother's house in Tennessee."

He quickly answered, "No, Leslie. You have gone viral."

"I am fine, really."

Was I being silly? Did I know what "going viral" meant in terms of the internet? I suppose I did. But in the context of the question, and with what was going on with the coronavirus pandemic, I answered to the best of my ability.

But I *had* gone viral.

Internet viral.

Millions and millions of followers. The irony of a sixty-five-year-old gay man acquiring this huge number has not been lost on me. I just love that folks want to hear what I have to say!

On my Instagram page, I usually follow the old rule of not discussing politics and religion in company. I don't know

HOW Y'ALL DOING?

what I don't know, and who would want to hear about what I don't know? All I know is comedy and my sweet self.

When our country was erupting in protests and marches, asking for the end of injustice against African American men and women, I was somewhat chastised by many of my followers for not speaking out against systemic racism.

That was the first time it really occurred to me that I had a voice on this new platform.

I had a strong voice. A voice that people wanted to hear.

I thought long and hard about what to say. Nothing I could come up with felt right. There might have been an easy way out. For me to say that my struggle was about my sexuality, about gay rights.

There is an old Southern expression: "I don't got a dog in that fight." But I immediately realized that was never going to be the case when it comes to standing up to racial injustice. We all "got a dog in that fight."

But this time, I just felt instinctively this was a time for me to listen.

Not talk, just listen.

Through a friend, I heard of a speaker, community leader and organizer named Deesha Dyer. She had been the White House social secretary for President Barack Obama from 2015 to 2017.

I watched a few of her presentations on the web and I was impressed. I reached out to her and wondered if she would be willing to take over my Instagram for a night. To talk about what was going on and what needed to be done.

Well, she was.

I announced on my Instagram account the next day that I really felt it was a time for me to listen. I asked each of my followers to come back that evening to hear an incredibly special speaker.

That evening, I turned my account over to Deesha Dyer. I gave her the liberty to say what she wanted with no restrictions.

I gave her the stage and the voice I had been given.

As you might be able to imagine, as I gained more followers, I also began to receive offers to push products. I made the decision I was not going to monetize this unexpected success during a pandemic. It did not seem right. I did not want my newfound friends to get the wrong impression about what my true intentions really were.

And that was to entertain.

That's what I do. That's my role. We all have different

roles in life. People come to my page for some FUN, not to see what TOOTHBRUSH I use.

Since my internet success began, things have changed a bit in my life. I have always garnered attention, but the attention over five million followers brings is much crazier!

I have a really cute BMW convertible I love to drive around in the California sunshine. Well, there's no more of that. People holler out my name and try to take my picture as I tool down the road.

I am afraid it might cause an accident! I drive with my top up now.

Here's another thing that has changed since I made over five million new friends. My favorite thing in the whole world is to sit somewhere, like Starbucks, and read newspapers. I read four newspapers a day. I read the *Los Angeles Times,* the *New York Times,* the *Financial Times* from London and *USA Today.* Snobby people sometimes ask me why I read *USA Today.*

Because I want to.

And because it is the only paper that almost all the hotels carry. I have just gotten used to reading it over the years, and the very sight of a *USA Today* newspaper gives me comfort.

Well, now all that sitting around reading newspapers in public places has stopped. People ask to take a picture with me, and I don't want to say no to anyone. And the requests are nonstop. Please do not for one minute think I am one of those famous people who grouse about the tedium of being well-known. But I feel badly for disrupting others who just want to sit and drink their coffee in peace.

I was fashionably late to the Instagram party, but I am having so much fun. I have found that my style of comedy works beautifully in short form. When I am putting together a post, there is a freeing quality to knowing I only have perhaps a minute to tell the story.

It has actually improved my comedic delivery.

Get to the point. Cut to the chase. No meandering around.

But, my friends, it has been writing this book that has given me true comedic freedom. Who knew that writing for the printed page could send an artist soaring? To be able to tell not only the story but the backstory as well. And the story that led up to the backstory. To find out how to segue here and there, and then segue back. To stray off into parts unknown.

And then figure out how to make it all track back and make sense.

I hope that each of you enjoys reading this book as much as I have enjoyed writing it. And if you are one of my friends on Instagram, know that you had a big part in this opportunity.

I do and always will consider you my friend. It brings me great joy to write about a life well lived in my daily musings.

Oh, and by the way, in case you are wondering, I use an Oral-B toothbrush.

THE TIME DEBBIE REYNOLDS CALLED MY MOTHER

Many years ago, I was honored to be involved in an AIDS event that raised millions for the cause. The event coordinators had the spectacular idea to pay respect to Bob Mackie, the renowned designer, by having dozens of supermodels parade down a runway wearing all his iconic designs.

When I first arrived in Hollywood in 1982, I had a fantasy where I wanted to be like a gay Hugh Hefner. I envisioned myself living in a huge mansion in the Hollywood Hills. And on Sundays, around my poolside lanai, I would have "brunches," which was a new word to me and something I had never attended but sounded really enticing.

Sunday "brunches." How very "tony." How very "au courant." These were other words I had started using with great affectation.

And in attendance at my brunches would be people like Bob Mackie. Mr. Mackie represented for me an upper echelon of successful, wealthy gay men that I clamored to be a part of. It was a glittery cut-glass ceiling I never quite broke through.

But now I was finally getting to meet him.

When we were introduced backstage, he was extremely sweet, but I think he had a million other things on his mind. He certainly did not fawn over me or act like we were going to be the best of friends.

But nevertheless, I was in gay-boy heaven. Just imagine what backstage looked like.

Bob Mackie designed for every gay icon known to man: Joan Rivers, Cher, RuPaul, Barbara Eden, Bette Midler,

HOW Y'ALL DOING?

Diana Ross, Judy Garland, Marlene Dietrich, Liza Minnelli, Tina Turner, Elton John, Ann-Margret, Carol Burnett, Marie Osmond, Diahann Carroll, Lola Falana, Carol Channing and Mitzi Gaynor.

And they were all there.

Well, maybe they were not all PHYSICALLY there. Maybe not even ONE of them was there. But they were all there in spirit as their gowns and costumes, carefully preserved, hung on dozens of racks, with all their jewels!

A feast of brightly colored outfits silently screaming to be worn down the runway by supermodels. Supermodels who were being attended to by legions of frenzied assistants grabbing and pawing while makeup artists painted pouted lips and hairdressers teased until every follicle in sight had been terrorized.

Pure pandemonium!

Look! There goes the Scarlett O'Hara dress from the iconic Carol Burnett skit! And look! The dresses from the opening number of *Dreamgirls* on Broadway! And look over there! Who wore that number? Was it worn by Mitzi Gaynor or Lola Falana? No, I believe it was Diahann Carroll.

Be still my foolish heart.

As the supermodels did their pony strut down the runway, the gowns and the costumes became more iconic and recognizable. With each offering, the primarily gay audience grew more and more frenetic and enthused.

As the hurly-burly was about to reach a fever pitch, I was pulled aside backstage. "Mr. Jordan, you have been so giving with your time and we are so appreciative, but we want to ask one more favor, and you can certainly say no. Mr. Mackie is expecting the dress with the headdress that Cher wore to the Academy Awards. But we thought it would be cute and funny to send you out first in another Cher costume. Bob will LOVE it!"

I was pulling off my clothes before they finished the last sentence.

We quickly settled on a bizarre French maid costume from the old Sonny and Cher show. My God, Cher must have been tiny back then. We struggled to shoehorn my fat little bottom into fishnet stockings and the exquisitely tiny maid costume complete with a perky little maid's cap.

For some unknown reason they threw black army boots on my feet to complete the ensemble. Honey, I was a mess. I looked torn up from the floor up.

But I hit the runway sashaying like Little Egypt, who "came out strutting wearing nothing but a button and a bow." I worked that runway like a seasoned veteran.

I swear, I outdid even RuPaul.

The crowd went BALLISTIC! It was a night I will always remember, but now I remember it for a slightly different reason.

I have identical twin sisters who are twenty-two months younger than me. They have run interference between me and my somewhat conservative Southern Baptist mother practically since birth. My sisters have always had their thumbs on the pulse of how my mother feels about certain things. They seem to know way ahead of me whether Mother will or will not be upset.

Soon after this event, one of them called in a tizzy. "Oh boy, Leslie. You have done it now. You are in this week's *National Enquirer* magazine. You know that is Mother's secret, don't you? Every Friday evening, she climbs in bed with a carton of butter pecan ice cream and reads that silly magazine cover to cover."

I was quite taken aback. "What on earth am I in the *National Enquirer* for?"

"It is just terrible. A huge picture, that takes up half the page, of you in drag!"

"In DRAG?!"

"And you do not even look pretty. You look awful."

Without even hanging up the phone, I ran to the nearest grocery store and grabbed the latest issue of the tabloid that can strike terror in the heart of anyone in the public eye.

There I was, big as life. Strutting along in my French maid costume.

And my sister was right. I looked awful. God-awful. The picture was taken at such an angle it was not clear I was ambling down a runway. I could have been strolling the streets of West Hollywood on my way to buy a carton of milk!

You must bear in mind this was years and years before *Drag Race* and other shows brought drag into the mainstream. Back then, "drag" was a purely gay phenomenon that when examined by outsiders seemed a bit, well, shameful.

There are those outside our community who cannot understand why grown men would want to dress up and lip-sync. Even within the gay community, the drag world has always been somewhat insular. There are gay men and women who love drag. They show up at all the shows and pay homage to their favorite performer by tipping dollar bills. It is almost like a religious ceremony. But there are other people who do not understand how outrageously fun and entertaining it is.

My churchgoing mama, back in those days, definitely did not understand!

I was actually brought out of the closet by drag queens. There used to be a wealthy doctor who had a big home

HOW Y'ALL DOING?

up on Missionary Ridge overlooking my hometown of Chattanooga. He would host "drag parties," which were heaven when we were underage and couldn't get into the one gay bar. We sure made use of those drag parties.

All the local drag queens took me under their wings. I stole a dress from a neighbor girl's house. It was a flowery hippie smock. I returned it covered in cigarette burns with lots of stains. The neighbor girl never did forgive me. Holds it against me to this day!

I was a messy drag queen.

We would stay out all night. I have no idea where Mother thought I was. I think I would sneak out the garage and have a friend pick me up around the block. The drag parties lasted till the wee hours. We would leave the house on Missionary Ridge and sneak down to Miss Odessa's Good Time House, a speakeasy in the Black part of town. Miss Odessa loved me. She would make me pork chop sandwiches at five A.M. I would sit there eating my pork chop sandwich looking really cute in my flowery hippie smock as the sun began to peek over the horizon.

I was given the name "Miss Baby Wipes" and could really bring the house down. I would lip-sync to "Mr. Big Stuff" by Jean Knight. I would jump up and do my drag number right in the middle of the living room at Miss Odessa's Good Time House. I think the denizens of this speakeasy were so inebriated, they had no idea I was not a real girl.

There was also a time during this period, when I was still underage, that I ran away to Atlanta and decided I could make a living as a female impersonator. I found out years later that my mother drove to Atlanta hot on my trail, sat outside a drag bar and watched me parade in and out in full drag.

She was heartbroken and too scared to confront me.

So, it is understandable that all these years later, when a picture of me in drag appeared in the *National Enquirer*, it brought back lots of bad memories. When I finally spoke to her, she was livid. "You live out there in West Hollywood where people can waltz around dressed like that, but I live here in Chattanooga, Tennessee, where such behavior is not accepted or tolerated. And for that picture to appear in the *National Enquirer*? It's just too much, Leslie."

I was gutted. When my mother was only thirty-three years old, my daddy's military plane went down. She was left with three children to raise. My daddy had been a take-charge kind of man who had always taken care of things. In the years following my dad's death, my mother began to rely on me. Even at eleven, it struck me how hard it was for her, having to handle everything.

HOW Y'ALL DOING?

Mother always seemed to be at a loss.

I remember once, she had been advised to purchase traveler's checks for some out-of-town trip we were taking. She asked me if I would go to the bank with her to figure it all out.

When we got there, she asked me if I would go up to the teller and ask how to purchase traveler's checks. I told her, "I'm just an eleven-year-old kid. You have to learn how to do these things now that Daddy's gone."

It seemed to make her mad. "I did not raise you to treat me like this."

But she walked up to the teller with newfound purpose. "Hello, my name is Peggy Jordan. And I am here to purchase traveler's checks."

The teller was in the middle of counting some money and did not even look up. "What denominations would you like them in?"

Mother hesitated. "Um . . . Baptist?"

A few years later, when I was fourteen, I told her I thought I was gay. I do not think I used the word "gay," as it was not in my lexicon. I was not even sure what it all meant. I just knew I was a queer.

She was flummoxed.

I think her only frame of reference for "that way" was perhaps Liberace, who never officially came out. Or maybe Paul Lynde as he sat there on the center square of *Hollywood Squares* making all kinds of snarky comments that seemed pointed in a direction in which no one wanted to go.

My mother did not pull out her Bible, which I thought was going to happen. She just looked right into my eyes and said, "Leslie, if this is the path you choose, I am worried you will be subject to ridicule. And I do not think I could bear that. Perhaps you could just live your life quietly."

I think, given her level of enlightenment on the matter, my mother expressed what she felt was best for me. I read somewhere once that our parents "did the best they could with the light they had to see with."

I love that sentiment.

And I tried to follow her advice. I tried to live quietly. Lord knows I tried. But my path became my path.

Just trust me on this one: it has NOT been a quiet path.

There were drug overdoses, hospitalizations, an arrest for shoplifting where she had to drive to Atlanta and bail me out, a death-defying bout with alcoholic hepatitis, and too many pleas over the telephone to wire money because I was "starving" to even count.

She bore it all with a great amount of fortitude.

And I have tried to make it up to her for the last half

HOW Y'ALL DOING?

of my life. Today, I am a good son. But through all of this, one thing has never wavered: how much I value her opinion on things. Because of the bond that the tragedy of my daddy's death secured, I have always valued her opinion above all.

Perhaps I valued her opinion too much, as this photo of me in the *Enquirer* was really just a silly transgression. And it had gotten blown way out of proportion. But all I knew was that my mother was upset with me and I could think of no way to remedy that.

That night, I attended a meeting at one of my myriad rooms of recovery. To my surprise and delight, I was seated next to Carrie Fisher. I had seen Carrie around the rooms for years and we had been introduced many times. I certainly did not count her as a close friend. But I think she picked up on the vibe that all was not well.

"You okay, kid?" She had always called me "kid." I was older than her, but it was a fun thing I reveled in.

My woes with my mother came pouring out. I told her the whole story and I felt a lot better for having shared. The phrase "Thank you for sharing" has become commonly used not only within the recovery community but in the outside world as well. I have even heard the term "oversharing" used outside of my recovery program.

But sharing stories of our lives and how alcohol and

drugs affected us really is the bedrock of the recovery movement—one alcoholic/drug addict sharing their "experience, strength and hope" with another.

And Carrie, bless her heart, listened attentively, which might have been a challenge as I tend to run on and on, forever and ever.

When the meeting was over, we were all having fellowship outside the front door and Carrie approached me holding out her cell phone. "Somebody wants to talk to you."

I put the phone to my ear and in that immediately recognizable, sweet voice, I heard, "Leslie, this is Debbie, Carrie's mother."

Debbie Reynolds was on the line!

I heard cartoon birds chirping and I expected her to break into song. "Tammy, Tammy, Tammy's in love!"

But she went right to the point.

"Carrie told me that your mother is upset with you because of some of the choices you made out here in Hollywood. Carrie told me she is upset from some picture in that awful tabloid magazine. I have been through the exact same thing. When that woman stole my husband . . ."

Okay. Okay. Deep breaths. Deep breaths. Am I really listening to Debbie Reynolds talk about Elizabeth Taylor's stealing Eddie Fisher away from her? Am I getting the inside scoop? I was just a kid from the suburbs of Chattanooga, Tennessee. I did not feel worthy. This was like a Hollywood exclusive. As Carrie Fisher pointed out in her brilliant one-woman show, it was today's equivalent of Angelina Jolie's stealing Brad Pitt from Jennifer Aniston.

Debbie Reynolds barreled on, ". . . and it was all over the press, my mother called from Texas and said, 'Debbie, I certainly hope that you are not considering divorce. You live out there in Hollywood where everyone and their brother gets divorced, but I live here in Texas and it is not accepted or condoned.'"

"Oh, Miss Reynolds! That is exactly what my mother said about me appearing in that magazine dressed in drag."

"Give me your mother's telephone number. I want to call her."

I was aghast. My mother is extremely private. I did not want her thinking I was airing our family's dirty laundry in public. But who in my mother's generation would turn down a phone call from the Unsinkable Molly Brown?

So, I gave Debbie Reynolds my mother's phone number.

All night and into the next day, I sat waiting to hear from my mother. Every time the phone rang, I jumped.

All this brouhaha made me extremely squirrelly.

When I had not heard from my mother by midday, I

finally took it upon myself to call her. She immediately jumped right in. "Leslie, what is going on?"

"Did Debbie Reynolds call you?"

"She's on my answering machine. But I thought it was a joke."

"It's no joke, Mother. I really want you to call her."

"Well, goodness gracious. Why?"

"She wants to tell you something."

"But when? When would be a good time for me to call?"

I had not thought of that one. "Let me call her daughter and find out a good time for you to call."

When I called Carrie, she laughed, "Before five o'clock. Five o'clock is 'kickoff time.'"

I told my mother the time and settled in for a long wait. Hours passed and I still hadn't heard anything. What could they possibly be talking about? I thought. What was Debbie Reynolds going to say to my mother about me?

Ring! I dove for the phone.

Mother immediately launched in without even saying hello. "Leslie, she's lovely. She is everything and more we have all believed about America's Sweetheart."

Debbie Reynolds told my mother she must not let anything I did in Hollywood be a reflection upon the way in which she raised me.

"Peggy, you must trust that he will do the best he can

to not embarrass you, and even if it does happen, you cannot hold him solely responsible. My daughter, Carrie, has told me that Leslie is a good egg, and my daughter, Carrie, is a good judge of character. Even though she sometimes loses sight of her own good character."

'Nuff said.

I was so grateful to Carrie Fisher for asking her mother to call my mother. It was a very fruitful conversation. It really changed my mother's view of my career and how hard it is to stay in the game, to stay relevant, to keep WORKING.

It was not until the conversation with Debbie Reynolds that my career choices began to make sense to her. I have never reached the pinnacle of an acting career, where you are allowed to make big decisions about what roles you'll choose. I've always taken what's offered and hoped for the best. Not all the roles I have played have been in the kind of shows my mother could brag and tell her friends about. I was raised in a home with very conservative family values. My mother is very protective of our family name. Anything I do reflects on that.

But somehow, her conversation with Debbie Reynolds opened a door. I began to talk to her about my misgivings about accepting certain roles.

We would discuss the fact that sometimes I picked

roles or opportunities not because I loved them or I thought the scripts were the most brilliant of my career, but because I needed the money, especially when I had an astronomical IRS bill and I needed to pay it off, fast!

We talk so openly about my career and my life in West Hollywood now. It has really changed our relationship. We have no secrets, and that is very freeing. I talk to her more now as a friend than as my mom.

And I really love to hear and trust what she has to say.

When it comes to moms, I won the lottery.

So here's a big thank-you to Debbie Reynolds and Carrie Fisher for making this all possible.

AMERICAN HORROR STORYTIME

I am the funny actor who comes in with the zinger. That is my job. I have been doing it for a hundred million years. I've even won an Emmy Award doing it. But, occasionally, certain writers, like Del Shores, David Kelley and Linda Bloodworth-Thomason, give me more to do and let me play a fully developed character.

But over the years, it is Ryan Murphy, the creator and writer of *American Horror Story* and many other shows, who has given me the most diverse range. I am still usually around for comedic relief and my parts are generally small, but Ryan has let me play some pretty deranged people.

And he loves to murder me.

In season six of the show, called *Roanoke*, Kathy Bates impaled me with a big wooden crook and pulled my guts out. The special effects people had a blast making a device that would shoot my entrails all over the place. They covered Miss Bates and me in fake blood, which consists of corn syrup and food coloring.

It is the most uncomfortable feeling I have ever experienced. Just imagine pouring a bottle of red corn syrup over your head and then letting it dry and get sticky.

After my fake entrails, yards and yards of them, were splayed on the ground and I was dead in the dirt, covered in corn syrup and food coloring, the director yelled "cut" and everyone ran to Miss Bates to make sure SHE was all right. Not one soul came to MY rescue.

Don't get me wrong, I adore Kathy Bates. It is just the nature of the business. The bigger stars get all the attention and the help.

Well, that is not entirely true. The wonderful actor Wes Bentley, who was also in the scene, assisting Miss Bates with my demise, asked me if I needed a hand up. Wes Bentley is such a sweet man. He pulled me up out of the dirt, as I was covered in that sticky fake blood.

Wes Bentley is so handsome. He is handsome like a

movie star. Oh wait, he is a movie star. He is my hero. And always will be.

Another time, a character named Piggy Man murdered me twice. And I think I still rose from the dead. Piggy Man had the head of a pig and the body of a human. I was so intrigued with the actor playing Piggy Man. I couldn't help but wonder who was under that disgusting pig mask. They had him dolled up in a tiny loincloth that left little to the imagination and he had a very lean, muscular physique.

It piqued my interest.

But alas, I never did find out who was under that Piggy Man mask in a loincloth. I have wondered about it for years now.

By the way, can I hear a big cheer for loincloths? I love them! It brought back memories of watching *Tarzan* every Saturday morning. At first, I was in love with Tarzan, but then as "Boy" got older, I fell in love with him.

And all the gladiator movies!

I'm not sure the gladiators wore loincloths. Their scanty attire was more like a pleated miniskirt. But the actors they hired were always so butch, they were able to make it work and not look ridiculous.

You must understand, for a gay boy of my generation,

all we had when our hormones got going was Tarzan, gladiator movies and the men's underwear section of the Sears, Roebuck catalog.

Can you imagine me in a pleated gladiator miniskirt? I would look like something from *Hullabaloo*, the dance show I religiously watched back in the sixties. Add white go-go boots and I'd look like I was ready to start doing the Pony.

Back to my story.

My first part on *American Horror Story* was in season three, which was called *Coven*. It was about a school for witches in New Orleans and also had something to do with the Salem witch trials. I played a witch on the Witches' Council.

I tried to figure out the whole interchanging plot, but I have a hard time paying attention. I was reading my script on my flight to New Orleans to begin shooting. I ended up just leafing through it, pink highlighter in hand and all the while muttering under my breath:

"Bullshit, bullshit, bullshit, MY LINE, bullshit, bullshit, bullshit, MY LINE."

I'm awful, aren't I?

I bet a lot of serious actors are clutching their pearls because I showed up on set having not read the whole script. But I have been at this game for over forty years.

HOW Y'ALL DOING?

And it's not that I've lost the zeal, I have just learned how to pull my weight without exerting myself too much.

Oh shoot, who am I kidding? I'm just lazy. And much too busy in my real life to do all that "an actor prepares" stuff.

Upon landing in New Orleans, I was immediately told the schedule had changed. I had to go straight to the set before even checking into the hotel. They were going to put me in my wardrobe and immediately begin shooting. I was told my scene was with Frances Conroy, Robin Bartlett, Sarah Paulson and Jessica Lange.

Wait. What? Jessica Lange?

And those other three brilliant actresses?

And I am unprepared? I had not even memorized my lines. Yikes. I was going to have to pull this one out of my ass. Soon enough, I was the one in my trailer forced to do all that "an actor prepares" stuff.

It was a whole blur as they got me ready and hustled me to the set. But all of a sudden, there she stood.

Miss Jessica Lange.

We were introduced and she was genuinely nice. Extremely sweet and accessible, which is a big compliment for someone as famous as her. She is real smart too. She was deep in discussion with a producer about a line in the script she had a problem with.

The line was: "If the glove fits, you must acquit."

This line was a take on the famous Johnnie Cochran quote from the O. J. Simpson trial.

As Miss Lange stated her case, I had to agree. The line had no place in this *American Horror Story* script. I am sure some overzealous writers were sitting around the writers' table and someone came up with it. And before they thought it through, it ended up in the script.

But then, for reasons unknown to even me, as I was not a part of the conversation, I blurted out, "I will say it. My character, Quentin, could say that line."

Right after I said it, I was a tiny bit appalled at my brazen request. But the producer looked it over and thought on it for a minute. He replied it was a possibility. He said the writers were already in the throes of a rewrite and he would pitch them my idea.

Oh my gosh.

I was to be given a line originally written for Miss Jessica Lange. This was EPIC. When we broke for lunch, I sequestered myself in my trailer to work on the delivery of the line.

My character, Quentin Fleming, was a smoker. They had me smoking unfiltered cigarettes. I had an aunt who smoked unfiltered cigarettes. She would take a big puff and then exhale. Sometimes, she would pick tiny bits of tobacco off her tongue as she talked. I know it sounds gross, but it wasn't. There was something very chic and cosmopolitan about it, like a writer in a French café.

I secured some cigarettes from the prop department and practiced with an unlit one.

"If the glove fits . . ." Then I would take a big puff. While I was exhaling and picking bits of tobacco off my tongue, I would deliver the rest of the line. ". . . you must acquit."

My delivery of this line was going to be a real show-stopper! It would be discussed in film classes and dissected by film scholars. But when we received the rewritten pages, my big line was nowhere to be found.

I swear, show business is going to be the death of me.

Oh well.

One thing I have learned during my years in Hollywood is that no matter how famous a person is, they are still just a person. Since I figured that out, most stars have disappointed me with their ordinariness.

But then there's Stefani.

Oh yes, Stefani Germanotta. Our Lady Gaga. She is in no way ordinary. And I'm not talking about her immense talent; that's a given. What caught me off guard, in a good way, was Stefani's unpredictability. With Stefani, you never know what is coming next. She's quite impulsive.

The gates are down, the lights are flashing, but is the train coming?

Maybe. Maybe not.

Within a few minutes of meeting someone, I can always tell how they were raised. It's just a matter of "please" and "thank you" and respect for one's elders. All that good stuff. Stefani Germanotta was beautifully brought up.

I am talking as if I know Stefani well and we are fast friends. Nothing could be further from the truth. We worked together on a few *American Horror Story* episodes from the season entitled *Roanoke*. Even though our job sounds quite glamorous, and there is interaction on the set with lots of laughs, when it is over, we go home. Just like you do after any other job. I certainly do not possess her phone number and have never hung out with her.

The episodes of *American Horror Story* we shot were a tiny bit befuddling. I never did, even after watching the finished product, figure out what was up. Stefani, whose character was named Scáthach, was costumed in an outrageous Pilgrim outfit, almost like rags. She was covered in dirt, with scary fake teeth and wild, unruly hair.

I was told Stefani's character was a wood nymph, a

sprite who was returning to avenge a gang rape on the *Mayflower* or some other ship of that era.

Are you with me?

I was mostly dressed in present-day clothing. My character was named Cricket Marlowe and I was a famous medium known for finding lost children. But I think I had been spiraled back in time or to another dimension. You would have to carefully dissect the script to find all that out.

Which I had not done.

In my big scene, my character was supposed to be out in the woods, scared out of his wits, stumbling along and holding a prayer card aloft. Then Stefani, dressed in her Pilgrim drag, was to jump from behind a tree and blow fairy dust in my eyes. Blinded, I was to fall to the ground and try to crawl away on all fours. Stefani was supposed to chase me, poking me with a stick, making fun of my talents as a medium.

"Can you see now, little man? Can you see now?"

When she caught me, she was to deliver a kick to my belly that flipped me onto my back; then she was to straddle me and cut my throat. Well, not actually cut my throat but brandish a knife, which would lead me to believe she was going to cut my throat. And then the scene was to end with her on top of me as we both delivered rather brilliant monologues paying homage to the Blood Moon.

Are you still with me? I understand if you're not.

It was an extremely complicated scene that involved a lot of rehearsal and lots of work with stunt coordinators to make sure of our safety. Plus, it was a night scene, which meant we'd start work in the early evening and then work through the night. Usually till the sun came up. I have never met an actor who does not abhor night scenes. It just throws your schedule completely off track.

You would not believe what is involved in getting the polished look of *American Horror Story*. We had smog machines to make it look spooky, dark and smoky. We had cameras on tracks so they could scoot along with us through the woods. We had humongous lights hanging up on sky-high poles to give the effect of moonlight through the trees.

And all of this for a scene that would probably play out for only a few minutes in the finished product.

But I was feeling the heat.

We were behind on the allotted time to shoot this scene and everyone was scurrying about to get it all ready. In the middle of these goings-on, Stefani asked me to step into the woods, as she wanted to talk to me about something.

HOW Y'ALL DOING?

About what? I wondered.

"Listen," she explained, "I tend to sexualize everything. Especially my acting parts. And I do not want to sexualize this character . . . but . . ."

And she stopped and pondered for a minute.

I remember thinking, Where in the hell is this headed?

She just stood there with her thinking cap on.

"Should we talk to the director?" I asked.

Stefani came out of her reverie and shook her head. A decision had been made. But before she had time to divulge what was going to happen, they began calling us to shoot the scene.

So we walked out of the woods and went to work.

ACTION!

With the fog machines making the woods look and feel creepy, I trundled along holding my prayer card in front of me for "protection." The cameraman and the guy who pulled the focus were rolling along behind me with the camera perched precariously on a track. They were practically breathing down my back. Plus, it was so dark and smoggy, I could barely see where I was going.

When Stefani jumped from behind the tree like a harridan, it genuinely frightened me. She blew the fairy dust into my eyes, but thankfully, it didn't burn, as whatever the prop department had come up with was innocuous.

I dramatically staggered backward holding my eyes and screaming. They had a furniture pad for me to fall upon, so I fell back out of view of the camera.

Once I landed and was off camera, the action was halted. Several people jumped in to remove the furniture pad and I settled onto the forest floor on my back. Then white milky-looking contact lenses were slipped into my eyes to give me a pitiful blind look.

ACTION!

As Stefani advanced, big stick in hand with harm on her mind, I rolled over onto my belly and tried to escape on all fours.

"Can you see now, little man? Can you see now?"

She kept poking me with the stick. I do not remember its saying anywhere in the script that the stick was to go up my ass, but she got awfully close. She then delivered the carefully choreographed kick to my belly and I was propelled onto my back with another carefully choreographed move.

Then she straddled me, and I had no idea what was coming next.

She began to ride me like she was in the rodeo. Her eyes rolled back in her head and she howled at the moon as she rubbed her nether parts with her hands. She became otherworldly. I was not sure what I was supposed to do! She produced the knife and got really close to my face, delivering her Blood Moon speech.

So I jumped in and delivered my Blood Moon speech.

CUT!

I lay there exhausted under Lady Gaga wondering, How do I get myself in these situations?

But apparently, the director and writers were thrilled with our performances, so even though it was three in the morning, they decided to build a platform several feet in the air for us to lie upon and repeat our monologues. The camera would then be able to get our faces in a more flattering position and with better lighting.

Or grab the money shot if Stefani decided to take it all the way!

Needless to say, it was a long, long night, but as I left the set with the sun coming up, I felt it was a job well done.

And it was mostly because of Stefani and her impulsive ideas.

Years went by before I was offered another part in *American Horror Story*, for *1984*. The first day I went to work on *1984*, I was in the makeup trailer and noticed the cast for this show was getting younger and younger. There was a really cute boy who was shirtless getting made up. Next to him was a little wisp of a girl, blond and adorable. They were chatting away. When they noticed me they both gave little yelps.

"We love you! You were so funny on *Will and Grace*!"

Unlike some actors, I love being recognized. It is nice to be appreciated for my work. Plus, I am just a show-off.

"I'm Gus, and this is Billie."

Oh my gosh.

Gus Kenworthy and Billie Lourd.

Now it was my time to yelp. Gus Kenworthy is a free-style skier turned actor. He won a silver medal in men's slopestyle at the 2014 Winter Olympics in Sochi. And Billie Lourd is the daughter of Carrie Fisher and the granddaughter of Debbie Reynolds, as well as being a really good actress on her own. Of course, with those genetics, how could she not be?

I immediately began to tell Billie my wonderful story about the time her mother heard my plight and asked her mother to give mine a call. Billie smiled and smiled. I'm sure everyone and their brother has a great Carrie Fisher or Debbie Reynolds story, but she seemed genuinely moved, as she had recently lost both of them.

I also told Gus how brave I thought he was to announce to the world he was gay in the midst of all his skiing success. And that I too had a dog named Beauregard.

He seemed thrilled that I knew all about him.

In the midst of all this, we heard a deep voice behind us say, "Well, this is just a real lovefest."

Dylan McDermott was in the room.

I have loved Dylan McDermott forever. He is in possession of that easy kind of masculinity that is so attractive to me and yet scares the shit out of me.

Why would butch men scare me?

Well, honey, it was not exactly a picnic on the playground growing up. I have learned over the years that the only really frightening behavior with butch straight guys happens when they are in a pack. They are like wolves showing off for each other.

They will do and say things they normally would not. They are like cavemen beating their chests. There is no telling what might happen.

That is when I am really at a loss.

But Dylan McDermott was just sitting there smiling and my heart skipped a beat. For the next few days, I was like a silly schoolgirl making up every excuse in the world to talk to him. He would sit with Leslie Grossman, the lead actress, whom I had also made a wonderful connection with, and they would talk.

Then I would pull up a chair and launch into my schtick.

I might as well have been beseeching him: "Look at me, Dylan! Look at me! Please, for God's sakes, pay attention to me! I ain't as pretty as Leslie Grossman but I'm witty and fun!"

Dylan and I began a silly flirtation that transcended the job and made it onto the internet. We would go back and forth. I named him King Daddy Ruler and I became the head of his make-believe fan club for middle-aged gay men.

And I put him at the top of my popular ever-changing list on Instagram: "Straight Men I Adore."

It was all nonsense but so much fun. And people on Instagram ate it up! We both gained many followers. And is that not what life is all about? Is that not the ultimate goal? Gaining followers on Instagram?!

I can remember a time in my life when a crush on a straight man would NOT have been fun. Not in the least. I took a pretty scary tumble into the netherworlds of codependency and unrequited love early in my sobriety.

If truth be told, it came to a head in sobriety, but I had suffered around these issues for YEARS. From the time I was in junior high school, I had been falling head-over-heels in love with boys who were completely unavailable.

Mainly because, duh, they were STRAIGHT.

HOW Y'ALL DOING?

It began as a game in my mind, a way to pass the time during a boring class in school. I would stare at the back of the head of the cutest boy in the class. And make up fantasies. We were dating. We were going steady. We would break up. We would get back together. It was all just a jumbled mess of feelings. And who in junior high knows how to deal with FEELINGS?

Oh, Lord. On and on it went.

I was certainly not out of the closet in junior high school. And I fought very hard to keep it under wraps. But I can say without any conceit, I was the funniest guy in school. I worked at it. Oh boy, did I work at it. And it was because of my sense of humor that I could befriend these straight boys and carry on our "relationships," which were all in my head.

We'd be grabbing a hamburger at the drugstore soda fountain after school and this unwitting straight boy would be doing just that: having a snack after school. I, on the other hand, would be on a "date." I had figured out what outfit to wear to school that day and worked on what we were going to talk about.

I would be witty and fun! Vivacious and becoming! Seductive and alluring!

And this went on for forty years.

FORTY YEARS.

Kinda pitiful, in retrospect.

Straight boy after straight boy. Crush after crush. And there were floods of tears and plenty of drinking to help ease the pain. Unless you've been in the throes of unrequited love, it's hard to explain how dark and dismal it is.

One thing I refused to consider, even though it tiptoed around in my subconscious mind for years, was that perhaps this behavior was wrapped up with the death of my dad. Maybe I wanted to find some kind of "daddy figure" to take care of me and protect me. And all the darkness around these crushes was a fear of abandonment, as my dad had died when I was so young.

Who knows?

When I was five years sober, I fell in love with a newcomer to my recovery program. It was hell. Developing feelings for or going after someone who is new in recovery is a big no-no. For all the reasons you can imagine. They are already crippled by the disease of alcoholism and/or drug addiction. They certainly do not need the drama of someone falling in love with them, but in their weakened state, they are fairly easy prey. And messing around with newcomers goes on quite a bit in the rooms of recovery.

But trust me, there are older members around the room who notice things and watch out for them. I was told in no uncertain terms to stay away from him. I was told this not only by my sponsor but by the sponsor of the newcomer.

There was something terrifying about having all this unmasked. It was embarrassing as hell. My mind is like a bad neighborhood. Honey, you do not want to go up there alone. I sought help both in the program and outside the program with therapists and such.

Thank God for recovery. Thank God for my willingness to face my issues head-on.

And thank God once I addressed the issue, I never looked back.

Why, you may be asking, did I wander off into a tale of codependency and unrequited love while telling you about my time on *American Horror Story*?

I'm not sure. Perhaps it is because I am taking my duties very seriously as the founder and guiding light of the Dylan McDermott Fan Club for Middle-Aged Gay Men.

Or perhaps because it was my own personal American horror story.

THE
SHORT
JOURNEY

We have all been told that life is about
the journey and not the destination.
Well, by the time I hit an age that could be considered
halfway through life's journey, I thought that was just a
bunch of pablum. I was not dealing with it very well.

I did not get to Hollywood till I was in my early thirties. But within ten years, I had pretty much accomplished what I wanted. My goal was to be able to live by
supporting myself as an actor.

Mission accomplished.

But after the glitter wore off, I felt like I was dog-paddling around just to keep my head above water. What was the point of all this? I had conquered television. I had been a part of a few award-winning feature films. I had even done a Broadway-bound play. The fact that it opened on a Friday and closed on a Saturday was not my fault!

But with all of that, I still had not quite found what I was looking for. I was too hip and young to even imagine this was a "midlife crisis." Oh please, how bourgeois. But something was up.

Over the years, I had somehow discovered that when I put pen to paper, it slowed my mind down to about the speed of how fast I could write, and I got clarity. Then I discovered, by reading some of my writings aloud, that my story and the way I put things was interesting for others to listen to. From there, I discovered I had a special talent. I could stand in front of folks and tell stories about myself, my life, my upbringing and, yes, my struggles, and people would be wildly entertained.

And more than willing to dig into their pockets to hear and see me and listen to what I had to say.

So I hit the road with a one-man show. I had a marketing firm in Palm Springs handle all the details, so all

HOW Y'ALL DOING?

I had to do was show up and spill the beans. My life became an endless array of airports, hotels and limos. Soon enough, I was at the top of my game and doing sometimes forty-four venues a year.

For a long time in America, people who have been discriminated against have created their own entertainment, outside of the mainstream.

Back in the day, African Americans had the Chitlin' Circuit. Jewish people had the Borscht Belt in and around New York's Catskill Mountains. We gays had our own circuit. There are clubs and venues in popular gay destinations all over the country. San Francisco, Key West, Atlanta, Dallas, Fire Island, Rehoboth Beach, Provincetown and all the gay meccas in between.

I performed in them all. Over and over again.

Try complaining to someone about your life when your life is this blessed and this big. But after years and years, the joy of performing was gone. I can say without any reservations that no one noticed. Anyone who works as a performer can attest to what I am saying. Especially those who have done long runs on Broadway, Off-Broadway and Off-Off-Broadway. I could walk onstage and bring the house down. Folks flocked to me after the show to tell me what a spectacular and moving one-man performance I had given.

But I was doing it by rote. Patter, patter, joke, joke, patter, patter, joke, joke, and bring it on home! Night after night. It was endless.

I am grateful that almost all this success came after I got sober. I can easily see how the seduction of drugs and alcohol can sneak in when a person goes from hundreds of people laughing and showing adoration to an empty hotel room.

Poor me. Poor me. Pour me a drink.

Just as I was stuck, feeling tired and sick of the traveling and the clubs, I took a short real-life journey that changed things.

It began with an early morning phone call.

"Hello?" I said into the phone sleepily.

"Pack an overnight bag and get over here. I've got something we need to do," she said.

"It's five in the morning," I snapped.

"Hush. I do not live by the clock nor the calendar. And neither should you. Pack a bag and get over here."

"Where are we going?" I asked.

"Never you mind. Meet me here at the house in a few hours. Hear me?"

"The house" was a splendid but decrepit mansion up in the Los Feliz section of Hollywood bordering Griffith Park. I had heard for years that this neighborhood was where the old money lived. Beverly Hills was for the new money, all the film-industry trash.

The house had been built by the Bullocks in 1903. They were department store people. And the person hollering at me over the horn was the current owner of the house, Miss Ronnie Claire Edwards.

Have you ever had a friend you cannot think of nice things to say about? Well, that was my friend Ronnie Claire. I cannot summon up bad things to say about her. I just cannot think of many good things to say about her. She has been dead and gone for years now and I do not want to disparage her name.

To tell you the truth, I adored her, but she was difficult, to say the least.

And she admitted it.

She told me once, "Dear, you know every family has one. That one family member that is just impossible. Well, in my family, it's me."

When I knew her, Ronnie Claire Edwards was a handsome woman of a certain age who hailed from Oklahoma City, Oklahoma. She jingled and jangled all over the place in big Western-style skirts, starched shirts with the collar turned up, espadrille sandals on her feet, hair swept up and out with a dramatic white streak like a skunk and bangles up to her elbows on both arms.

She was beyond chic and did not care "what Paris has to say." She had her own look and was not to be deterred.

Her daddy had been a well-known defense attorney back in Oklahoma City. The stories about him were legendary. He once drove a judge to such distraction, the judge yelled in exasperation, "Mr. Edwards! Are you trying to show contempt for this court?!"

Mr. Edwards calmly replied, "No, Your Honor, I am trying to hide it."

Mr. Edwards sent his daughter off to seek her fortune with these profound words: "Ronnie Claire, keep your dress down and your legs together."

His daughter inherited her daddy's biting tongue. One time, we were discussing a famous actress who was internationally known for her beauty. Ronnie Claire had a different opinion. "I cannot bear to look at her, Leslie. She has that tiny pinched face that looks like it is not quite done. Like it needs to go back in the oven for ten minutes on high."

Ronnie Claire is best known for playing the character of Corabeth, the snooty shopkeeper, on *The Waltons*. But her money did not come from acting. She had married a Texas millionaire when she was young. She left him to pursue her acting dreams, but years later, out of the blue, he died and left her millions. She bought that big man-

HOW Y'ALL DOING?

sion up in Los Feliz and lived there for twenty years with a succession of Jack Russell terriers, all named Sister, for company.

Well, she was not always completely alone. For a few years, she had a boyfriend, but he lived down in the basement. His name was Stanley and he had at one time been a big deal on Broadway. I'm not sure but I think he was in the original production of *Company*. He had a phenomenal singing voice and was as handsome as a movie star, but he died young.

It was whispered that the first time Ronnie Claire allowed Stanley to perform a certain sex act, to "mill around down there," as she offhandedly put it, he had stood butt-naked on the bed and sung the entire "Hallelujah Chorus."

I often wondered why Stanley had not lived in the house. My gosh, there was enough room. There were five empty bedrooms! When I asked Ronnie Claire why Stanley did not live upstairs with her, she shrugged and said, "Dear, the key to a good relationship is the key. Give me back the key."

Oh well, so much for the "Hallelujah Chorus."

Later that morning, after our early morning phone call, I pulled up to the house and there stood our other running buddy, Jane Abbott. Jane Abbott is a Texas gal and intrinsically the funniest human being I know. She was a perfect foil for Ronnie Claire's acerbic tongue.

When Jane's poor mother had heart surgery, Jane was trying to explain to us that the doctors had inserted a valve from the heart of a pig. Ronnie Claire sniffed, "Well, I just hope she doesn't begin to root for food."

My favorite story about Jane Abbott happened when she was in college in Lubbock, Texas. At the time, there was a flasher who was known to throw open his jacket with nothing on underneath. This pervert would knock on doors in the girls' dormitory, then flash whoever answered. Jane answered the door once and there he stood, ready to flash. Jane immediately hollered, "Wait! Wait! I gotta get my glasses!"

She is a big, fun, loud Texas gal with a heart of gold.

As I parked, Jane leaned her head through my car window. "You been roped into this, too?"

"I can't say no to her. I have tried for years. Where are we going?"

"Lord only knows."

At that point, Ronnie Claire gunned the engine and backed her vintage Jaguar out of the garage with the tires shrieking.

We hopped out of the way and jumped into the car, and off we went.

HOW Y'ALL DOING?

Riding in an automobile with Ronnie Claire Edwards at the wheel was an exercise in terror. She rarely stayed in her lane. She never kept her eyes on the road or her hands on the steering wheel. And she talked incessantly, gesticulating like an amateur thespian. How she did not notice the number of horns blown in her direction is a mystery to me.

"Before we hit the road, pilgrims," she barked as she pulled into the filling station on the corner, "I gotta get this old girl gassed up."

Suddenly, she started laying on her own horn. I was appalled. "This is not full service, Ronnie Claire. This is a self-service gas station. We have to do it ourselves."

"Two things I don't do, dear, is bring myself to an orgasm and pump my own gas. They'll be out here eventually," she said, blaring the horn some more. All the while she tapped her fingernails on the side of the car and peered impatiently out the window over her white 1950s cat-eye sunglasses.

A young sheepish cashier came out eventually. He did just as Ronnie Claire told him. That happened a lot. People always seemed willing to do Ronnie Claire's bidding. It just made things easier.

As we barreled along the highway, all I could get out of Ronnie Claire was that we were headed to a town called

Death Valley Junction. It was explained to me that Death Valley Junction was established in 1907 by the T & T Railroad. But the last train had headed out of town in 1940. Ronnie Claire, a rabid reader, was a font of information.

We traveled for five hours.

Her Jaguar had a faulty air-conditioning system, but Ronnie Claire was not about to spend a penny on that old car. She did not even have air-conditioning in her house. I think she had a window unit upstairs in one bedroom but that was it. And rather than heat the house, she wore floor-length mink coats all day long in frigid weather.

"Frugal" does not begin to describe Miss Edwards. She had more money than God, but we used to laugh because she would have elaborate dinner parties and serve chicken thighs cooked with figs. Why? Because chicken thighs are the cheapest cut and she had fig trees growing in her backyard, all free for the picking.

While we hurtled along the road into Death Valley, it was so hot, I thought I was going to be sick. Jane and I hung our heads out the windows to at least get hot air on our faces. It reminded me of when I was little and the whole family, grandparents and various aunts included, would pile into a woody station wagon and drive to Daytona Beach for summer vacations. Us kids had a mattress in the back, but even with all the windows open, it was still stifling. We would strip down to our underpants.

Not the adults. Just us kids.

As Ronnie Claire, Jane and I pulled into town, the only thing still standing was the Amargosa Opera House and Hotel. It was beyond help, a ramshackle building, its paint peeling, and hard to see in the afternoon sun. There were tumbleweeds rolling down the street, just like you see in the old Western picture shows.

We got out of the car and stood, stretching and staring all around. The silence was deafening. Everything shimmered and glimmered in the heat. For some reason, it reminded me of the one time I regrettably took an LSD trip in college.

I wondered how anyone could live comfortably in this heat. An old man who looked like a rotten crabapple wandered out to help us with our luggage. I did not get too near, as I was concerned he might stink.

One whiff of bad body odor and my day is ruined.

Inside, sitting very erect at the front desk, was an old woman with her hair pulled tightly back in a ballerina bun and a slash of red lipstick that did not stay within her God-given lip lines. The funny part was her attitude. You would have thought she would be overjoyed to have guests, but she lorded over us as if she could not be bothered!

Ronnie Claire would only spring for one room with two beds and a foldout. When we got to the dismal room, I voiced my opinion. "I am going to sleep on top of the covers with my clothes on. This place creeps me out."

"Well, I gotta unhook this bra before I die," lamented Jane as she reached up under her cotton top and did just that. This had happened many times before. Jane could whip that bra off in ten seconds flat. She always struck me as amazingly comfortable in her own skin. She is a pretty girl but not a raving beauty. She is a big girl, what some people call "big boned." She has always seemed perfectly comfortable with what nature gave her.

I began to whine. "What are we doing here anyway, Ronnie Claire? Where are we going to eat out here in the middle of nowhere? I am famished."

Ronnie Claire, who was circling the room like a panther, checking it all out, replied, "Just you wait, little man. We got some big plans lined up. They are going to feed us soon."

At dinner, things began to look up. We had the dining area of the hotel to ourselves and were waited on very quietly by the only two people in town, the elderly couple.

During dinner, Ronnie Claire remained mum about

the purpose of this trip. Afterward, she led us out of the dining area and into the Amargosa Opera House next door. We were stopped in our tracks when we saw the interior of the building. I could tell by the look on Ronnie Claire's face that she, too, was surprised.

The interior of the opera house had been beautifully restored. It looked like the inside of a precious jewel box. There were totally unexpected, glorious murals hand-painted on the walls. The murals were of a Renaissance audience deeply enthralled by the performance onstage. They looked frozen in time.

We were led to our seats by the same old man, who thus far had dutifully performed as the bellhop, the waiter and now the usher. We were the only three people in the audience and it was a Saturday night.

From backstage, we heard the shuffling of feet, and a disembodied female voice filled the auditorium from a creaky old sound system. "Our first pantomime involves a young girl who anxiously awaits her lover at the train station. Will he show or will he not?"

Canned music began and the olio slowly rolled up to reveal an ancient ballerina en pointe. It was the motel receptionist!

What began to unfold was a conundrum that defies the imagination.

As the aged ballerina careened about, the old man joined her onstage in various disguises. He shuffled here and there like a deranged Charlie Chaplin. I garnered that he must have been playing the train station operator, the disapproving father and the lover.

But none of it made sense. It was just a bunch of ham on rye.

On and on it went.

It was endless. Pantomime after pantomime. Hours and hours. I think they were both so overjoyed to have a small semblance of an audience, they pulled out their entire repertoire.

When the self-indulgent lovefest ended, we sat there awkwardly, not knowing if we should hang around to greet the "artists." The problem was solved as the prima ballerina assoluta came forth to the front of the stage. But once again, instead of graciously thanking us for coming, she stared down her nose at us.

She even held out her hand as if we were supposed to kiss it.

In the room after the performance, Ronnie Claire was finally ready to spill the beans. She told us the woman's name was Marta Becket. About forty years ago, Marta and her husband had been driving west from New York

HOW Y'ALL DOING?

and had a flat tire near this ghost town. Marta wandered through the town and spotted the empty and derelict opera house. She ended up buying it and set about fixing it up. She actually hand-painted all the murals herself.

"Here is the kicker," said Ronnie Claire. "The olio goes up week after week with or without an audience. And she has been doing so for years and years."

I asked her how she knew all this.

"I read about it in *National Geographic* magazine."

We talked into the night about the phenomenon we had witnessed. This performance, which was mediocre at best, had so embedded itself into our subconscious. There was something incredibly noble about Marta Becket and her husband's performing for years with little or no audience.

After we stopped talking and as I lay there waiting for sleep, it occurred to me how important it was for me to continue performing my stories. I had been given a gift. It was God-given and I needed to use it. The fact that the thrill was gone from performing my stories was irrelevant. Witnessing someone like Marta Becket performing just for the sheer joy of doing it changed the way I thought about my career.

This wild, unexpected short journey had completely renewed me.

Marta Becket is gone, but I am still out there performing. Sometimes up to forty-four venues a year. Some nights, I feel it. Some I don't. But I keep at it.

Nightly, I stand offstage, outside of the spotlight, waiting.

"Ladies and gentlemen, you may know him from his Emmy-winning turn on *Will & Grace*. You may know him as the Tammy Wynette–obsessed drag queen in the cult-favorite feature film *Sordid Lives*, or from his frequent roles over the years on *American Horror Story*. And let's not forget his gobsmacking success on INSTAGRAM . . . please make welcome . . . LESLIE JORDAN!!!"

Then I walk out to thunderous applause and into my light.

WARHOL CAPOTE

After my dad died when I was eleven, I remember that I had a lot of trouble sleeping. My mother would let me sit up late and watch television. My program of choice was Johnny Carson. With all his interesting and famous guests, his show seemed like a window to a life I was fascinated by but knew absolutely nothing about.

Boy, did it beckon to me. I bet those glamorous people did not live in the boring suburbs and were not dragged to church every time the doors opened.

One night as I was glued to the tube, Truman Capote prissed out onstage like an aging show pony. He had a long scarf tied around his neck and giggled like a shy schoolgirl. Johnny Carson seemed amused and did not seem to be taken aback by Truman's effete manner.

But I was horrified.

I had already been teased at school about my somewhat effeminate manner. And being the son of an extremely masculine father only seemed to enhance the issue. Somehow his death mixed it all into a rather heady cocktail of shame.

As Truman minced and lisped through his appearance, I had trouble watching him. I went into the bathroom and threw up. He scared me to the core of my being. I felt there was something shameful about Mr. Capote's posturing. You could see it in the eyes of people in the studio audience. Grown men were not supposed to act like that.

The only other person I knew who had behaved in this manner was the organist at my church. He was a "confirmed bachelor" and a favorite with all the little old ladies. They loved him and fawned all over him. They were always baking him cakes and casseroles. But even at that young age, I could feel the awkwardness when the men of the church were forced to be around the fey organist.

Was this a mirror of what I was going to become? Was this what being "gay" meant? Would I be like the organist or like Mr. Capote and make the men I knew uncomfortable?

HOW Y'ALL DOING?

I had no one to ask. No one to confide in. I was all alone in my misery.

But being the industrious sort, the very next day, I took a bus to the Chattanooga Public Library. I began reading everything Truman Capote had written. It was as if I was looking for clues to what it all meant.

I did not have one inkling about what "it all" was.

I soon devoured *Other Voices, Other Rooms*. Everything about that book floored me. Especially Joel's distaste for Randolph, the mysterious old kimonoed queen who lived upstairs, even though Joel began to realize they shared a common bond of both being "different."

At least that is what I read into it.

Somehow, in the thrall of all those offbeat characters so wonderfully drawn and brought to life—the red-headed hellion Idabel, elegant old Zoo and Jesus Fever, crazy Miss Amy, brokenhearted Randolph and of course Joel and his interactions with all the goings-on—things began to somewhat make sense in my young mind.

I've always thought the beauty of Mr. Capote is that his work can be interpreted so many ways. He never hits the nail on the head. He just wanders around it with a beautiful vagueness.

But I knew.

I knew what was going on. Underneath it all.

I somehow segued into the plays of Tennessee Williams, which were also filled to the brim with "veiled implications." I knew what Skipper and Brick in *Cat on a Hot Tin Roof* were up to.

It left me breathless.

Poor Maggie. She did not stand a chance!

I read everything there was to read about and by Truman Capote and Tennessee Williams.

Ever since that one night watching *The Tonight Show,* Mr. Capote has tiptoed around my subconscious.

In Cold Blood started my lifetime fascination with true crime. Mr. Capote was ahead of the curve. True crime is now a staple of television and films, not to mention all the books that have been written and become bestsellers.

But *In Cold Blood* read like a novel.

I was and am hooked on anything to do with true crime. I do not like scripted shows about crime. I don't even like it when the true crime shows use actors to replicate the true crimes. I want to see "talking heads" who were involved, and I especially love it when the murderer is interviewed behind bars.

Human nature is really on display in these types of programs.

When *Esquire* magazine published four chapters from

HOW Y'ALL DOING?

Capote's unpublished novel *Answered Prayers* in 1975 and 1976, I thought I had died and gone to heaven. What a shockingly heady read that was!

I certainly did not run in Truman's circles of the rich and famous, but I was in the same frame of mind at that time in my life. Truman Capote expressed how it felt with such verve. It was an exhilarating but very tumultuous time for gay men. This was all in the days before the AIDS crisis, so we had no limits on the sex and the partying.

I was like a bag man in a limo back then. I never knew where I was going to end up, so I carried a bag loaded with my basic necessities and stuffed with a couple of cute outfits to wear to the gay clubs. The party was never ending.

I was lost. We all were and did not even know it.

Through it all, Truman was constantly in the news, thick tongued and staggering about with all the beautiful people, a cocktail in his hand.

Years later, after his death, my name began to be bandied about to play Truman, but nothing really came from it. There were Broadway plays about him and several movies where apparently my name was brought up, but none of it came to fruition.

Then, when I was in my early sixties, I received an offer

to portray Truman in a play. The two-character play, called *Warhol Capote*, was centered around a true-to-life story about the friendship between Truman and Andy Warhol, the infamous pop artist. This Broadway-bound production had the pedigree of a top Thoroughbred race-horse. I was so honored to be included.

It had all started when Rob Roth, the award-winning director and self-proclaimed Andy Warhol aficionado, reread *The Andy Warhol Diaries*. While rereading, he spotted several references to an idea that Andy and Truman had for a Broadway play about the two of them.

When Andy Warhol died, he left behind three thou-sand audiotapes. Long before the days of social media's keeping a log of everything we think and say, he was recording his life on his Sony Walkman. Many of these tapes were labeled "Truman."

Rob Roth approached the Andy Warhol Foundation to see if he could give them a listen. At first they refused; the tapes could not leave the foundation. There were also lots of stipulations in Mr. Warhol's will about when the contents could be divulged.

Then Rob received a rather clandestine phone call from one of the Warhol board members. He told Rob that his idea of writing a play about the artist and the writer was spectacular, but the board would need more nudging. It was suggested he approach Truman Capote's heirs, who might be more open to the idea.

Perhaps after, they would approach Andy's heirs.

There was a lot of back-and-forth between the estates. But all the people entrusted with the legacy of two such towering artists were intrigued.

Finally, the Andy Warhol Foundation came to Rob Roth with a list of demands. What they were asking was somewhat outrageous. Since the tapes could not leave Pittsburgh, Rob would have to hire someone to transcribe eighty hours of recordings. When Rob was told the cost of an audio transcriber, he almost fainted. But with further research, he found a transcriber right there in Pittsburgh who was willing to work within a reasonable budget.

It resulted in eight thousand pages of transcript!

It was then up to Rob to pore over all those words—the actual words of Andy Warhol and Truman Capote yammering away, sometimes in "altered" states of mind. His difficult task was to not only make sense of the transcript but to also organize it into a coherent play.

After a few years, he thought he had it down.

When I first read the play, I was a little worried. Not about the material, oh no; the material was awe inspiring. But I was looking at sixty-eight pages of dialogue. Although Andy was not known for his verbal gymnastics, sometimes, out of the blue, he would drop these really great verbal bombs. Truman was the real blabbermouth. How on earth was I going to memorize all those words? Not only did I have to memorize almost seventy pages of dialogue, I also had to say them in Truman's legendary accent and cadence. People forget sometimes that memorizing lines is a big deal in stage work. Those who can do it easily have a gift.

I am not one of those actors.

The older I get, the scarier it gets. When you flub in front of the camera, it can be done again and again until you get it right. Not so onstage. If you forget your line, it is up to you to find it in the recesses of your mind and bring it forth!

It's the scariest feeling on earth, to be in front of an audience and "go up," as we say in theater lingo. There you are, in the spotlight, floundering around trying to ad-lib your way back to sanity. And no one can really help you. Sometimes fellow actors can whisper the line or make up nonsense lines to help you remember, to try to lead you back.

But mostly it's just up to you.

And it's hell.

Truman himself had a reoccurring nightmare that he was onstage but could not remember his lines. He once told Gloria Steinem, about his dreams, "I walk onstage . . . but I just stumble about, mortified."

I learned Andy Warhol was to be played by Stephen Spinella. When I first heard his name, I could not place him, but I knew it seemed familiar.

Well, no wonder.

When I looked up his filmography, I saw he had worked more than any actor on this planet. My God. Pages and pages of projects he had been in. The list was endless.

And I thought I had worked a lot!

I once looked myself up on IMDb Pro to see all the parts they had listed for me. It was astounding. There were 386 shows I had been in.

Some of them I did not even remember.

Added to Mr. Spinella's list of accomplishments were two Tony Awards for his performance as Prior Walter in the renowned Tony Kushner play *Angels in America*. Not ONE, but TWO. He received his first one for part 1, *Millennium Approaches,* and the next year, he won another Tony Award for part 2, *Perestroika.*

Warhol Capote was to be directed by Michael Mayer. My goodness, talk about top-drawer! He had won a Tony for directing *Spring Awakening* and had been nominated for a million other Tonys. Being an actor who resides and mainly works in California, I had no idea how limited my knowledge was of New York theater. When Michael Mayer and Rob Roth began talking, I felt like they were speaking a language I did not understand.

They were both fans of me and my work and had talked in depth with me about this project, so I am not sure why seeing them in action, on their home turf, threw me into such a silent tizzy. They just seemed like such "big-city boys," so in-the-know about things I didn't know diddly squat about.

Like opera. What do I know about opera? I swear, I think Michael was leaving soon to direct an opera in Beijing or Parts Unknown. Out there somewhere. They were all agog about it, but it just rendered me mute.

Add the accomplished Stephen Spinella to the gabfest and I felt like the apple in the old grammar school question: what does not belong among two oranges and an apple sitting on the table?

We began rehearsals in New York in a large loftlike studio. It looked like something you'd see in the movies. Behind a long table sat a million people, and there were stacks of the script and a million sharpened pencils standing at attention.

There were certainly not a million people, but there were a lot of them. And there were a lot of pencils. Who were all these people? And what were they going to do with all those pencils?

And then the real fun began.

Michael Mayer pulled out a pair of scissors and Rob Roth went white. He knew what was coming. Michael felt Rob, having worked on this project for years, had lost objectivity. Michael felt that much of the play did not "track" in a cohesive and understandable manner. He cut the script into ribbons and laid the ribbons all over the floor. Michael began to put speeches and such into groups. When he would put a ribbon aside, Rob would squawk. Michael would assure him that he was not getting rid of anything, just rearranging things.

On it went for days.

I began to slowly panic. You see, when I had first gotten the script, long before we began rehearsals in New York, I had begun to commit things to memory since I am such a slow study. I had taken the script and highlighted all my lines. Any time I had a line lasting longer than three sentences, I deemed it a speech.

Then I counted. I had thirty-three speeches to learn, and I slowly began to memorize these speeches.

Now, horrors of all horrors, the director was taking scissors to all the speeches.

In the midst of all this, we loaded up the show and moved to Boston, where we were going to open at the American Repertory Theater. ART is the theater at Harvard University. I cannot tell you how amazing and awe inspiring it felt for this little Tennessee boy from the suburbs to stand in the Harvard student center and get a lanyard with his name and photo. I bought a T-shirt, too, to prove it. I was considered a member of the Harvard community now. I wore my lanyard everywhere.

Even in the shower.

I would look into the bathroom mirror stark naked and tell myself, "How do you like them apples!"

But things slowly went sour.

It's so hard to think back on a time when I feel like I failed. If you questioned anybody involved with the production, I doubt they would say I failed.

But I feel like I did.

The biggest realization came when I discovered I am not the kind of actor who can disappear into a role. I will never be a Robert De Niro or a Meryl Streep, an actor who can disappear into the parts they play. And trust me, this disappearing act involves more than wigs and assuming an accent. It is a gift I'm not sure I have been given.

There is just a whole lot of ME. There is just too much of ME to disappear.

HOW Y'ALL DOING?

I'm more along the lines of a Dolly Parton. What you see is what you get!

Would I be able to disappear into Truman Capote, whom I was beginning to somewhat dislike? There is no denying his talent, but he was rather despicable. He was certainly witty, but his wit always came with a bite. Especially when he drank. I think he was desperately unhappy.

Before I left Los Angeles, I had begun working with a speech therapist hired by the production to help me find Truman's speech patterns. Truman had a speech impediment. It was deemed a lisp, but if you listen closely, it is not a lisp. I could not parrot his sound. I tried and tried. I listened to tape after tape. I even tried, on the advice of the speech therapist, to watch his mouth in slow motion. The thought was that if I could move my mouth like his, I could produce the sound of his voice easier.

Even that did not help.

The day before we had our first preview audience, it came to a head. The show was now in the hands of "the Two Dianes," as I affectionally called them. Diane Paulus was the artistic director and Diane Borger was the executive producer at the American Repertory Theater.

They are both lovely ladies and whip smart. They had already taken many of their productions to Broadway.

But we had a problem on our hands. I could not remember my lines. And I could not seem to replicate Truman's speech patterns. It was decided that perhaps we could put a "feed" in my ear and have someone offstage give me my lines.

It was a disaster.

There was an urban legend floating around for years involving Carol Channing and Mary Martin. The two ladies were doing a play called *Legends!* on Broadway. Mary Martin had trouble remembering her lines. So, the story goes, they placed a feed in her ear. But this technology was in its early stages and the feed kept picking up taxi dispatches near the Broadway theater. Miss Martin would repeat the dispatches, driving poor Carol Channing to distraction.

"We have a pickup at Fifty-Third and Broadway."

The problem for me was not the feed in my ear; it was the logistics of how a line should be fed to an actor onstage. There can be no pauses while the actor onstage listens to the line to be repeated.

I had a theater professor who once put a metronome onstage. Then he would sit in the darkened theater and snap his fingers in time to the metronome. It was to keep the actors onstage moving the words along. His theory was, theater is a heightened reality and the language must

Baby Leslie! Mama was the baby of seven, daddy was the baby of three, so when "the babies" had a baby it was quite the occasion!

Mother and me on the Jersey Shore right before we sailed to meet my daddy, who was stationed in Germany.

My favorite photo of all time.
My daddy, Allen Bernard Jordan,
with the three of us. He doted on us!

Christmas, when we were little,
was the best! In choir robes my mom
made for the Christmas Cantada
at Central Baptist Church.

The county fair was always a highlight.
Especially the baby farm animals
exhibits.

My senior high photo!
I wanted to be a hippie.
I look like a serial killer.

On the set of a TV pilot titled
The Road Raiders starring
identical-twin bodybuilders
named The Barbarian Brothers.

My twin sisters, my mother and me (affectionately known as mama and them) celebrating the holidays in Chattanooga, Tennessee.

Throwing out the first pitch at the Washington Nationals game in Washington, DC, for Pride Day in June 2016.
Shutterstock

Me with a racehorse. Some of the happiest memories of my life!

Riding a horse in LA!

Entering the famous Sound Emporium music studio in Nashville to record my album *Company's Comin'*.

Standing in "the Circle" at the Grand Ole Opry in Nashville just before making my Opry debut.

Lunching with Katie Couric in Los Angeles.

Meeting Dolly Parton for the first time and getting on my knees to present her with a gift.

Dolly Parton and I posing for a holiday photo that I can give to Mama.

My dear friend Eddie Vedder and I at dinner in Los Angeles. Eddie and his family are some of the finest people I know.

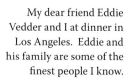

snap. In film, actors can meander around the line, but if there is a pause onstage, it should be a pregnant pause. A pause with meaning. A pause that says something.

So there I was, onstage, with a feed in my ear and a theater student feeding me my lines. In order for me to listen to each line, there were a lot of pauses. The pauses, I'm afraid, made me seem "slow." Well, Truman Capote was a lot of things, but he was certainly not mentally slow.

I feared impending doom. Mainly because, well, doom was impending.

The feed sealed the deal. It was so humiliating. I could not speak the words even when they were spouted into my ears. It became a nightmare that would not end.

On the fateful day before our first preview, Diane Borger invited me to lunch. She was so empathetic. She asked if there was anything they could do to help me. I knew instinctively where this was headed and so did she.

I think it saddened both of us. I think it saddened all involved.

But we had tried everything. I had spent hours and hours running the lines with an assistant stage manager. It was all to no avail. Once onstage, dressed to the nines and looking just like Truman, I would panic.

Nothing came out of my mouth.

Michael Mayer even suggested that I carry a notepad

and read my lines. I just felt this was a desperate attempt by the director to save the show.

At rehearsal the following day, I asked the stage manager to bring everyone to my dressing room for a meeting. When all were assembled, I crumpled. I remember I was leaning against a wall and I just slid down it and sat despondently on the floor. But it was the love in that room, for both theater in general and for me as a person, that allowed me to say the words that needed to be said.

"I do not have this in me."

There was an inaudible sigh of relief from all gathered. They all knew this, but I needed to be the one to say it. They immediately jumped into action. The previews were put off for a week and they hired another actor to play Truman. He was flown in immediately and in one week had to learn the entire play. His name was Dan Butler. They had no idea of the history that Dan Butler and I had.

Years and years before, in Los Angeles, Dan and I had both been volunteers for Project Nightlight. It was an organization dedicated to the idea that no one should die alone. This was all in the middle of the AIDS crisis, and because of the stigma attached to the disease, family and friends walked away, leaving the AIDS patient alone. When a patient went into a hospice program, Project Nightlight went into action.

HOW Y'ALL DOING?

One evening, my phone rang late at night. It was Dan Butler. "Leslie, I need some help. I am at an apartment in Hollywood with a guy who is really close to making his transition. He was raised by his sister and brother in North Carolina. They are here now, and I know this sounds silly, but their accents are so thick, I can barely understand them."

I ran over to a rather seedy place near downtown Hollywood. It was a night that I will never forget. The guy died, and from our training, we knew what to do. The brother and sister were so grief stricken, we had to do most of the organizing. We called the assigned mortician to come get the body, but before they arrived, we removed all the medical equipment from the room. We lit candles, we opened windows, and we changed the patient's clothes. We even shaved him, as his siblings wanted him to look nice. I found out they were all Southern Baptists, so we sang some hymns as well.

About a year later, Dan Butler took me to lunch and told me he had a one-man show coming up. It was opening Off-Broadway in New York. He asked me if he could tell the story of that night as me. I was a little befuddled, but I agreed. When I saw his performance, though, it was magnificent. He actually BECAME me. My voice, my mannerisms—it was uncanny. I was genuinely touched and so honored.

And now, years later, he was replacing ME to do Truman Capote.

Go figure.

As I had booked other work and had to get back to Hollywood, I was unable to see a performance of *Warhol Capote* at the American Repertory Theater starring Stephen Spinella and Dan Butler.

But I heard it was sterling.

By the time I walked away from the play, I was not in any way upset about the whole ordeal because I had learned a valuable lesson. I had learned to not be afraid to try things because I think it might not work out.

I think that fear keeps so many of us from being successful at things outside our realm of experience. We love to stay in our comfort zone, but the growth only comes when we wander outside of that zone.

I learned so much about acting and about myself from the experience. After all those years, all that time, the very last thing Truman Capote taught me was that there was no shame in saying "I do not have this in me."

I guess maybe I do like Truman a little more than I thought.

NOT
IN MY
HOUSE

We used to gather. Way back when. Us gays.

Every morning, we would gather at the Starbucks in West Hollywood, the one across from the Sports Connection on Santa Monica Boulevard, or as it was called back then, the Sports Erection.

We gays are not a glum lot.

We have fun names for all the places in WeHo. The swimming pool at our recreation center is the Gay Pool. The nearby dog park is the Gay Dog Park. Starbucks is Gaybucks. The hardware store is the Gay Hardware Store.

Gay this. Gay that. Gay everything.

Gay. Gay. Gay.

So, there we were, all gathered, one gay sunny California morning at the Gaybucks. I was sitting at a table near the door, and although the place was full, things were quiet and orderly.

When suddenly the door burst open and three rowdy boys clanged in, one of them dragging a bicycle. They were trouble with a capital T. One look and I knew.

They were rough trade.

The term "rough trade" has always been bandied about in gay circles. It can cover a lot of ground. It usually summarizes a lower class of rent boy. But it can also cover a breed of boys who sit at the bar entertaining gay patrons for drinks like big, ugly escorts. Most of these boys are straight. How can that be? you might ask. Honey, I could write a whole book on "gay for pay" and what all that entails.

Just trust me on this one.

I have always had a fascination with the underbelly of life. Before I got sober over twenty-two years ago, I was a bar drinker. I was the kind of drunk who sat at the bar for hours calling the waitress "Nurse" as I begged for another round.

Lord knows, back then, I could easily have credited

HOW Y'ALL DOING?

myself as "the founder and guiding light of the Leslie Jordan Home for Wayward Boys."

A friend of mine sitting near me saw my interest in the boys in Starbucks that morning. "Chipped teeth, tattoos and dirty fingernails. Right up your alley, darling."

"Uh-uh, no, ma'am," I answered. "I do not vibrate on that frequency anymore. Too old now. Too much drama."

The three boys were raising a ruckus when they came into the establishment and were already causing a commotion at the cash register. The saucy little queen who managed the Starbucks had seen them coming and was "sitting on ready." Apparently, they tried to pass a credit card that was flagged as stolen.

"Out!" the manager said, pointing to the door. "Just get out of here and I won't call the cops."

"First, give me my card back," one of the hoodlums demanded.

"Oh no. No, no, no. This card is stolen. I'm keeping it."

The hooligan flushed a deep red. "That card ain't stolen."

"Get out or I will call the cops."

"That card ain't stolen. Give it back!"

As the situation escalated, one of the three started surveying all the other patrons. The whole place was staring with fascination at the scene that was unfolding. Angrily, he burst out with a real zinger.

"What are all you FAGGOTS looking at?"

Dead silence. Our mouths agape. Emboldened and really digging the attention pointed his way, he proceeded to spout off. "Oh yes. Lots and lots of FAGGOTS in here. FAGGOTS everywhere."

He pointed to the person nearest to him. "You're a FAGGOT."

And then to another. "YOU'RE a FAGGOT."

And then he came to me. "And YOU are an OLD FAGGOT."

I came up out of my seat loaded for bear. "OLD?! Who are you calling OLD? Now, you listen to me. You need to shut your mouth and get the hell out of here."

"You need to shut up and take a seat, FAGGOT."

I stood right up to him. I took a deep breath. I spoke slowly with great conviction. "Oh no. No, no, no. Not here. Not in my house."

In retrospect, I have wondered repeatedly why I was not scared. This guy could have pummeled me. He could have made mincemeat out of me in a minute. Plus, he could have been packing some heat. He could have shot me dead. You read about stuff like this all the time in the paper.

But he touched a nerve in me that ran deep.

See, when I got off the bus in Los Angeles in 1982, I planned to pursue a career in show business. But something more pressing came my way. I got off the bus downtown, but I quickly found my way to West Hollywood.

Honey, there were queers everywhere. I had come out of the closet in my early twenties, when I lived in Atlanta. But I had always dreamed about a place like West Hollywood, far from the Deep South, far from the Southern Baptist church I grew up in. I landed in this fabled Southern California city with a resounding thud and I dropped anchor.

But West Hollywood in the 1980s was a city in crisis. The AIDS epidemic was ravaging the population. When the gay community realized we weren't going to get help from the government, we knew it was up to us to take care of our own.

From the very beginning, I was a part of this quest to meet the crisis head-on.

My first volunteer job was delivering free meals to homebound AIDS patients for an organization called Project Angel Food. It was in its infancy when I came on board. There were chefs who donated their time and volunteers who helped distribute the food. They were cooking in a small kitchen, located in the upstairs portion of a church on the corner of Fairfax and Fountain in Hollywood. All of us who had volunteered to deliver the food were given four hot meals and four addresses.

For some unknown reason, I was given the La Crescenta route, which is really far out in the boonies. La Crescenta is about seven miles from where Christ lost his shoes. And that, my friend, is FAR.

By the time I reached my first house, the food was already cold. But more important and pressing seemed to be the condition of this homebound patient out in the wilds of La Crescenta. He seemed to have nobody to look after him. He told me that a caseworker came to check on him but was so harried from all her other patients she rarely stayed longer than twenty minutes. He was starved for human attention. I ended up staying for a couple of hours. I even changed his diaper, which was certainly not listed in my Project Angel Food volunteer job duties.

I was eventually told I was being relieved of my delivery duties as there were complaints of the food's being cold. I was flabbergasted. "You mean I'm being fired? You can't fire me. I am a volunteer. And I'm doing the best I can."

They began to reassure me immediately and gently guided me to another organization within the fold they felt was more suited for me. It was a brand-new program called Project Nightlight.

The beginnings of this organization were rather auspicious. A nurse named Cassandra Christenson, who had primarily worked with dying cancer patients, was walking through the Miami airport when she bumped, quite literally, into Mother Teresa. Mother Teresa was a Catholic nun who dedicated her life to caring for the sick and the poor. Her order opened a hospice for the dying lepers in Calcutta, India. When Cassandra Christenson bumped into Mother Teresa on that fateful day and told the tiny nun she was a nurse who worked with terminal patients, Mother Teresa gave her a calling.

She said, "Have you heard of AIDS? We are going to need a lot of help with people suffering from AIDS."

Cassandra began the work and founded Project Nightlight. Its goal was to make sure anyone who went into a hospice program was never alone unless they wanted to be. We would sit and listen to the patient. We would sit and read books aloud. Most important, we would sit with them all night long.

I was a part of this wonderful volunteer program for many years. From it, I learned one of life's biggest lessons: true happiness can only come from being "of loving service to others."

Especially those in the last throes of life's journey.

West Hollywood was the center of it all for the Los Angeles community in the fight against AIDS. The beauty of all this—and yes, you can find beauty even in a crisis—was that we came out of this dark period a much stronger and more loving community.

So, I suppose that when this disrupter called me names in the West Hollywood Starbucks, where we had all worked so hard to make a safe place for gay people to live and to die, it struck me to my very core.

I stood tall and said, calmly and evenly, "I have taken nonsense like this my whole life. But not here. Not in my house. Do you understand me? You really need to go."

He backed down immediately. I think he recognized the passion behind my words. He motioned to the other two and they skulked out the door without another word.

Suddenly, I came to my senses and all the blood rushed to my head. I thought I was going to faint. I stood there trying to collect my wits. Several people gathered around patting me on the back and thanking me.

As I tried to calm down, I saw, out of the corner of my eye, the same guy who had called us that awful name, spitting on the window and glaring at me.

Without a moment's hesitation, I grabbed my gigantic Starbucks cup of sweet iced tea and stomped toward the door with my newfound friends begging me to stop and to not do anything rash.

HOW Y'ALL DOING?

Well, I didn't listen to them. I flew out the door and slung my iced tea right in his face!

Everything stopped. I think it startled me more than him. He slowly wiped the tea out of his eyes and held his hands up. He knew exactly what to do. By not reacting, by not striking back, he held all the cards if the cops came.

And did they ever.

The manager of the Starbucks had called the West Hollywood sheriff's office when things began to escalate. This kind of incident, leaning toward homophobic, is something that the West Hollywood sheriff's department did not want.

Soon enough, I counted ten cop cars, all from the West Hollywood sheriff's department, sirens blaring, flying to a stop around us. Why on earth was there this kind of reaction to something so minor? I suppose it was because West Hollywood had become a real tourist mecca. Our annual Halloween street festival was drawing thousands and thousands of people from all over the world.

The three boys who had caused the trouble seemed to know their way around an event of this nature. I certainly did not. I was appalled. And I was also scared about my involvement. When you work in the public eye, things like this can always be misconstrued and taken out of context.

I could see the headlines in my mind's eye:

GAY SITCOM ACTOR LESLIE JORDAN INVOLVED IN WILD FRACAS IN WEST HOLLYWOOD.

GAY SITCOM ACTOR LESLIE JORDAN HURLS ICED TEA IN A BLIND RAGE!

THAR SHE BLOWS! GAY SITCOM ACTOR LESLIE JORDAN GOES ON A RAMPAGE!

As the police were questioning people and putting the three rowdy boys in the backseats of three different police cars, I called my best friend in DC, Mike Lotus. He works for the Secret Service and I thought he would know the proper way to handle the situation.

He advised me to keep the dramatics to a minimum and make sure they knew I felt threatened before I hurled my iced tea. He stressed the importance of remaining calm and rational. I was mulling all this over when a policeman pulled me aside.

"Mr. Jordan. You know that we could arrest you on the spot. According to the witnesses, including the assailed, it seems that you initiated the altercation."

"Threw the first punch? I'm not butch enough to throw the first punch!"

I went off on a rampage. My attempted calm and rational demeanor went scampering away. I might as well

HOW Y'ALL DOING?

have been Bette Davis hollering, "But ya are, Blanche! Ya are in that wheelchair!"

You have never heard such histrionics. The high points of my impassioned speech revolved around the fact that the rough boy was mean to me, the rough boy called me names, the rough boy had frightened me out of my wits. I was just trying to protect myself.

Plus, I told the cop, if I went to jail, there would be four thousand deeply disappointed homosexuals, as I was leaving the very next morning on a gay cruise to Alaska where I was the comedy headliner!

And then for my final flourish, I dramatically turned around and put my hands behind me. "But if you must, arrest me. Arrest me. Throw me in the slammer. I will tell my story to the judge."

I stood with my back to the cop for a moment or two.

When I turned back around, he said, "Are you done? Mr. Jordan, you are being overly dramatic. This has been resolved. We talked to the three combatants and they have agreed to stay out of this area. They are being released and you should go home and calm down."

I looked over and the three guys were walking down Santa Monica Boulevard. As I was watching them go, the one I threw the sweet iced tea at turned around, pointed at his eyes and then pointed at me. He was letting me know he had his eyes on me and I'd better watch my back.

I thought my bowels were gonna let go.

How do I get myself in these situations? I knew I would have to walk around scared to death he might find me and beat me up. Good Lord, I am in my sixties, but it was like I was eight years old and back on the playground.

Sadly, I stayed away from the West Hollywood Starbucks for a while. I relocated to another one down on Melrose Avenue. It had more of a hip crowd as opposed to the gay crowd. And then one day, I was sitting sipping my iced tea surrounded by Melrose Avenue hipsters and I thought to myself, This is ridiculous. I am not going to stay away from a place I dearly love and enjoy because of fear.

So I got into my car, drove to that West Hollywood Starbucks and promptly ordered a sweet iced tea. And I continue to go there to this day.

I never did see that boy again. I heard a rumor that he and his cohorts in crime tried the same trick at a Starbucks up on Sunset Boulevard and were once again caught in the act.

There is nothing worse than a stupid criminal.

We are taught in recovery to pray for anyone we have a resentment against. We are supposed to get on our knees and pray the person gets the blessings in life they desire.

HOW Y'ALL DOING?

Oh brother.

I did as I was instructed. I prayed and prayed and prayed for that awful boy who called me those awful names.

It did not help. My resentment was not lifted.

I am just a rolling ball of resentment, and I'm okay with that.

Because you don't do that in my house.

HYMN SINGING

I come from a long line of hymn singers.
For generations, my family has sat in pews singing hymns, sat on riverbanks singing hymns, swung in swings on front porches singing hymns. We have sung hymns in barns, in the backyard, on picnic benches and at family reunions. We have sung hymns while ironing our clothes, cooking our food, mowing our grass, hanging our laundry on the line, feeding our animals and shining our shoes.

Hymns were sung when we were born, hymns were sung when we got married and hymns will be sung when we are put in the ground.

"Will the circle be unbroken, by and by, Lord, by and by. There's a better home awaiting. In the sky, Lord, in the sky."

My daddy, Allen, and his older brother, always called Mack Junior, along with their cousin Jackie Reece, would pull out a guitar or a baritone ukulele at any family gathering and go to town. A lot of the songs were silly ditties that had been passed down generation to generation.

"My daddy was a-shavin' as the story goes. The razor slipped and it cut off his nose. The doctor sewed it on but sewed it upside down. Now every time it rains my daddy nearly drowns. If you don't believe it, don't blame me, I'm only tellin' you what my daddy told me!"

Or sometimes, they would sing popular songs they had heard sung on the radio. I was really surprised at their stirring rendition of Bob Dylan's "Blowin' in the Wind." Daddy taught me all the chords on my baritone ukulele, and I learned to play and sing it as well.

Another favorite of mine was "Kumbaya, My Lord." It was always sung around campfires when I was a kid. There is something incredibly comforting about the song. The word "*kumbaya*" means "come by here" in the language spoken by the Gullah, African Americans who live on the islands of South Carolina, Georgia and Florida. The song is easy to sing, as it repeats phrases such as "Someone's singing, Lord" or "Someone's laughing, Lord" or "crying," or "praying," or "sleeping." Then comes the "*kumbaya*," which is basically beseeching the Heavenly Father to "come by here."

HOW Y'ALL DOING?

But eventually, we would always end up singing hymns. We would all sing hymn after hymn. From the youngest grandkid to the oldest grandmama or granddaddy, the hymns burst forth.

We had a good time.

I have been blessed with a family that loves to laugh and loves to tell funny stories. I've seen families out in restaurants where they eat a whole meal, and no one says a word. Well, that ain't my family. We are all big talkers, big laughers and big storytellers.

And we all fight just to get a word in edgewise.

We also love jokes. My daddy was a master at telling jokes. They were never dirty. Just questionable. He was a real cutup and the funniest person alive. I loved his Dumb Dora jokes.

"Dumb Dora was climbing a tree. All the boys laughed and pointed up. They told Dumb Dora they could see her underpants. Dumb Dora was no fool. To show those boys, the next time she climbed the tree, she didn't wear any underpants."

I didn't really get it, but I would laugh and laugh.

Poor Dumb Dora. You could not get away with Dumb Dora jokes in this day and age, that's for sure.

My dad died while on active duty in the army, so he was to be buried at the Chattanooga National Cemetery.

We were all in the funeral limo on our way to the burial site. Knowing that there would be a gun salute and not wanting us kids to be frightened, Uncle Mack Junior launched into a joke.

He said, "Kids, here's a good one I heard the other day. The whole family was gathered at the burial site for a beloved granddaddy. He had died in service to his country. So, when the guns went off for his gun salute, it startled his wife so much, she flipped backward out of her folding chair and lay spraddled on the ground. One of the grandkids jumped up and hollered, 'Oh Lord, now they got Grandma!'"

A little dark in the joke department, but we kids thought it was hilarious. Imagine the surprise of the fellow funeral-goers when my family fell out of the limo laughing uproariously as we were about to bury my daddy.

But that's just the way we were. We always thought it was better to laugh than cry. There is not much of the family left on either side. It is just down to me, Mama and the twins. No heirs at all. No one to leave my millions to. Oh, wait. I ain't got millions.

But we still have a good time.

HOW Y'ALL DOING?

"Joshua fit the battle of Jericho, Jericho, Jericho. Joshua fit the battle of Jericho. And the walls came tumbling down . . ."

I get my sense of humor not only from my daddy, but also from my mother's daddy. His full name was Homer Howard Griffin. No one ever called him Homer; he was always H. H. My grandmother called him Howard.

My mother was in the sixth grade before she figured out the Lord's Prayer was not, "Our Father who art in heaven, Howard be thy name."

He was well up into his nineties when he died. He kept his sense of humor to the very end even though he went a little batty. He would sit all day long in his easy chair and pull imaginary strings down from the ceiling. It was as if those strings were attached to balloons. But there were no strings and no balloons. We weren't quite sure what he was up to.

Then he would holler at my grandmother, who was always in the kitchen cooking, "Mary Lucille, the baby's crying."

His off-kilter behavior exasperated my grandmother to no end. She had borne him seven children and they had been together for a million years. She was not about to put up with his silliness. She would come flying from the kitchen, scissors in hand. She would cut whatever imaginary string Granddaddy was pulling down from the ceiling and holler, "Howard, we haven't had a baby in this house for fifty years!"

Then she would stomp back into the kitchen muttering under her breath about how crazy he was. I'd look over and Granddaddy would wink.

I never did figure out if his nutty act was for real or just to get Grandmama's goat.

These are memories that last.

Memories that linger.

"Blessed assurance. Jesus is mine. Oh what a foretaste of glory divine!"

The way I was raised, we went to church every time the doors were open, and hymn singing was an integral part of my church experience. I honestly believe if I had not been born homosexual, my experience with the church would not have ended the way it did.

I found great comfort in the church as a child and I wanted to be an exemplary Christian. I wanted to follow the teachings of Christ to the best of my ability. I think that if things had been different, I would still be in the church singing hymns. But as I got older, I could not reconcile my beliefs with the religious teachings of the church on homosexuality.

So at seventeen years of age, I walked away.

And the hymn singing stopped.

Well, that is not entirely true. I do vaguely remember some hymn singing one rowdy night in Knoxville, Tennessee, when I was in college. I was doing some out-of-control drinking with a group of gay men. As we got drunker and drunker, we realized that each of us had the same story. We had all been raised in the church and we had all walked away because of our innate sexuality.

Somehow we ended up out on a balcony singing hymns at the top of our lungs with our arms thrown around each other. We all knew every word to every hymn. But what had been a rowdy, joyous occasion suddenly, as so often happens with inebriated people, turned on a dime into a sad, tearful night.

Can you imagine the spectacle of sobbing queens on a balcony drunker than Cootie Brown? We must have been a sight. Those damn hymns still had a major grip on us!

But mostly, the hymn singing stopped.

And the years rolled by.

Leslie Jordan

My friend Mike Lotus, who works for the U.S. Secret Service, is always searching for outlets to exercise his creative side. I imagine it serves as a nice outlet from demands and stress of his profession.

A few years ago, he and I came up with an idea for a musical. It was to be called *Church! (A Spirited Revival)*. I wanted the musical to take place in a traveling tent revival in the Deep South. I thought it would be hilarious to have a preacher who was obviously gay as Christmas but completely closeted. He has a very unscrupulous wife and an adopted son who pretends he is deaf and mute. They go town to town basically bilking congregations out of their hard-earned money. He preaches, she sings and then they trot out the son and "miraculously" heal him. After the offering plate is passed, they count up the take and move to the next town.

It was decided that I would handle the creative end and Mike would use his skills producing. We approached our mutual friend Travis Howard to write some music for us. Travis is a successful country music writer and producer. He decided to include another successful songwriter named Danny Myrick. Between the two of them, they've

HOW Y'ALL DOING?

written songs for Dierks Bentley, Tim McGraw, Miranda Lambert and Jason Aldean, just to name a few. And they wrote some phenomenal songs for our musical.

My love of church music and my love of these old hymns began to resurface after so many years.

But after several workshops, as so often happens, we realized that the music far outshone "the book" and we put it aside until we could find the right playwright to map out a script that would do the music justice.

In the midst of all this, Mike Lotus, who grew up a devout Catholic outside of Chicago, fell in love with church music from the South. Travis Howard has a successful Instagram Live on Sunday mornings that showcases not only his music, but many of the hymns both he and I grew up with in the church. At Mike's direction, Travis and I recorded some of these hymns and we put them on Instagram.

I think it is important to remember that my explosion on Instagram was the result of a pandemic. This pandemic shut the whole world down, including churches and all houses of worship. My decision to sing hymns on Sunday was not a result of churches' closing their doors, but more a result of my mind trying to find a resting place from all the chaos in the world.

But the songs were so beautifully received!

It was almost as if our hymn singing was filling a void for folks who were not able to go to church and sing with their loved ones. I was shocked at the overwhelming number of positive comments.

"My grandmother is dying, and this brought me so much comfort."

"This was my father's favorite song and it brought back such wonderful memories. Thank you."

"I am an atheist, but I love these old hymns. I hope you never stop singing them."

"Listening to your hymns is like my own private Sunday service."

So in the midst of all this positive reinforcement, and at the request of my newfound friends on the web, the decision was made that I would make a gospel album. Travis would orchestrate the music and I would sing.

I do not consider myself a good singer, even though I have sung and performed in choirs my whole life. But two things I noticed after hearing a recording of my voice when I was singing: my voice still sounds like I am from East Tennessee, and my voice sounds unique singing these hymns. I think it is because these hymns are the very fabric of my being.

HOW Y'ALL DOING?

"When the roll is called up yonder, when the roll is called up yonder, when the roll is called up yonder, I'll be there."

When we began working on the gospel album, we started putting together a wish list of who I could sing duets with. At the very top of my list was Dolly Parton.

I have loved Dolly forever and ever.

Amen.

When Dolly Parton's first big smash single, "Jolene," came out in 1973, I could not quit singing that song. And I was not alone. There was something so relatable about her pleas to the other woman to not take her man.

It was a really heartfelt song, and it was such a catchy tune.

I was living in Knoxville at the time, so I decided that I would drive up to Pigeon Forge and see Dolly Parton in concert. When we were kids, Pigeon Forge was just a stop on the road to Gatlinburg.

I cannot for the life of me remember where she performed. I'm fairly sure it was in the high school auditorium.

Of course, this was way before Dollywood.

This was also before Dolly transcended country music and became a big movie star, way before she was known worldwide. But she was already Dolly to the core. She had lots of funny jokes that she worked into the show in between her songs. My favorite was when she patted her hair, which was teased up real high, and said, "What's a country girl without her haystack?"

Then she sang "Jolene" and we all cried. She sang "Coat of Many Colors" and we all cried.

I get emotional just thinking about it.

In the fall of 2020, I met her "go-to guy" through my mutual friends, Gary and Larry Lane. His name is Steve Summers, and he is the creative director at Dolly Parton Enterprises. The list of things he does for Dolly is endless. He acts as her stylist, he designs all her sets, he is a lighting expert and travel planner and helps organize all her events. When he heard of my deeply felt desire to meet Dolly, he arranged it all.

And let me tell you, it was beautifully done.

I had told him all about my dream to have Dolly sing a duet with me on an album of hymns that I was in the midst of doing. He had seen me on Instagram singing hymns and threw the idea out to Dolly. She readily agreed.

I almost fainted when I got the news. Was I really going to be recording a hymn with Dolly Parton? If you had told me this news a year ago, I would not have believed it.

He told me the best way to go about it was to go into the studio, make a "scratch demo" using the best musicians we could find, lay in my vocals and then send it his way. He said Dolly likes to lay in her vocals in her own studio. Well, it sounded like a really good plan. We found out quickly that the world's best session musicians are in Nashville.

So, off to Nashville we went.

With Mike Lotus, Travis Howard and Danny Myrick spearheading the whole shebang, we hit the recording studio at the iconic Sound Emporium. The song they selected for Dolly was "Where the Soul of Man Never Dies." The musicians they hired worked from "charts," which means that the various notes were written down but each musician took those notes and riffed on them with their various instruments.

It was magical to behold.

To hear each and every musician add to this heavenly cacophony of sound, to hear a song unfold and build, was breathtaking.

We were told that Dolly was doing a short interview for *Entertainment Tonight* at another studio in Nashville and we were welcome to drop by and say hello. I was just beside myself. A fantasy I'd held for thirty-six years was about to come true. It was pouring rain when we arrived. We were met by Danny Nozell, her manager, and escorted into the studio.

And there she was.

She was in the middle of her *Entertainment Tonight* interview, so we could only see her through a tiny glass window. But it was a perfect way to see Dolly for the first time. Framed like a teeny tiny little doll. She was dressed in black leather from head to toe.

She was like crème brûlée. You wanted to eat her with a spoon.

When she finished her interview, we were brought in to meet her. It was a tiny bit awkward as our masks were a must. My first words to Dolly were about figuring out if we could take our masks off or not. It was decided that even if we were "social distancing," it was still a good idea to keep the masks on.

Since meeting Dolly, I have been asked repeatedly, "What is she like?"

And my response has remained the same: "Well, you know exactly what she's like."

I say this because Dolly is exactly like you think she would be. She is gracious. She is sweet. She is smart as a whip. And she seems right at home in any situation.

The world is a better place for having Dolly Parton in it.

And I, personally, want to emulate her. I want to live a life where no one can say a bad word about me. Because I have never heard a bad word about Dolly. Folks may or may not like me, but they certainly will not be able to denigrate me.

Because I plan to live my life asking myself constantly, "Well, what would Dolly do?"

Now, years have passed since my family sat around rooms, instruments in hand, singing hymn after hymn. Many things have changed, the family has gone and my own relationship with these hymns has transformed.

But these songs will always be in my blood. They are a part of me, as much as my blue eyes or my height.

After all this time, I'm truly proud to say that I am a Jordan, and I am a hymn singer. There is nothing fancy about that. There is no wealth, no rich upbringing, no inheritance. But what I was given is much more important than that, something that money cannot buy. I was given good Southern manners, taught the difference between right and wrong, given a sense of family and community, given faith in humanity and in a God that can move mountains.

Yep, I am a Jordan, and I am a hymn singer.

THE PONY FARM

Since I was a little boy, I have wanted a pony farm. It's a dream that has been with me through all the seasons of my life.

I never actually used the term "pony farm" until a few years back when I was invited to a party in the Hamptons, the ritzy enclave at the tip of Long Island, outside New York City. The party was at a property called the Pony Farm, which is exactly what it used to be.

When I arrived, I was enthralled. It still had little barns and white-fenced paddocks. But no ponies. The ponies were from a bygone era. As everyone drank and ate all the marvelous food, I stood by a window, staring out at the barns and paddocks, dreaming of the farm I might have someday.

When I was five or six years old, I started making scrapbooks filled with pictures of ponies and horses that I cut from magazines. I cannot remember a time when I was not fascinated with horses and ponies. The first TV show I remember watching was a Western starring Peter Graves called *Fury*. It was about a horse named Fury. The young star was a kid named Bobby Diamond. With the help of my mother, I sent him a fan letter and got a signed picture in return. I also loved watching *My Friend Flicka*, which was also about a young boy and his horse.

My daddy once took me to a barn owned by the local chapter of the Shriners. They had a whole pasture filled with Shetland ponies. I was allowed to go into the pasture and pet them all.

I was hooked with the first pony I petted. So the dream began. I wanted a bunch of ponies, not just one.

I cut out photos of barns, pictures of fencing surrounding the pastures and paddocks. I cut out pictures of tack rooms and feed rooms. I cut out pictures of haylofts. I cut out pictures of anything remotely related to horses and ponies.

My dad bought me some fencing, and I would nail the boards to the trees at the top of our property to make paddocks for my ponies, who were only pretend ponies at that time. I also made gates going in and out of each paddock. I would gallop all around, sometimes pretending to ride the ponies and sometimes just becoming the ponies.

It was my own little world. I was so lucky to have parents who fostered all my imaginary goings-on. I think it is what has made me a good writer and actor today.

I am a superb pretender!

I had absolutely no problem playing by myself. I did once allow this rather alarming girl in my neighborhood to join me in my pretend games. But she embarrassed me at our elementary school Play Day by galloping like a horse instead of running like a human at the races.

I didn't play with her anymore after that. I mean, really, it's one thing to pretend to be a galloping horse in your own backyard, but to do it in front of the whole school?

Rather embarrassing, don't you think?

Then one Christmas morning, I ran into the living room and under the tree was a tiny pony saddle. I was perplexed. My mother's brother, Norman, worked at a saddlery, so I thought maybe this was a present from my uncle.

But why a saddle and no pony?

Then it occurred to me that maybe, just maybe, there was a pony, but Santa Claus could not get the pony down the chimney. I ran to the window, and standing in the backyard in the snow was a fat, black Shetland pony. Santa Claus had had the good sense to cover this pony with a warm horse blanket. The horse blanket was too big and swamped the pony.

He looked a bit comical. But to me, he was the most beautiful thing I had ever encountered. His name was Midnight, and he was with me till I was almost fourteen years old.

We were an average-income family. I think most people might think having a horse or a pony is a big extravagance. And I would imagine in today's world, it would be. But back then, it was not. Especially in the South, where land is plentiful and there are barns all over the place.

My parents were really young and energetic.

When I got Midnight, we lived in the suburbs. Our backyard was fenced in, but it was just chain link. Not the kind of fencing I fancied for my pony. But it was good enough to keep him in the yard while he grazed. And there was lots of grass for him to eat.

HOW Y'ALL DOING?

Daddy and I built a small shed for the pony to stay in on cold nights. Daddy put a couple of heat lamps in the corners and we piled it high with straw for Midnight to sleep on. He was immediately right at home, especially when we filled his manger with sweet feed and tasty alfalfa hay for him to eat.

I do not know where Midnight came from or how he had been treated before I became his owner, but as soon as he came to the Jordan household, he was living high on the hog. And I was the most popular boy in the neighborhood. I have often wondered, looking back on all this, if the neighbors had a problem with my having a pony in the backyard. I mean, after all, ponies do poop a lot, and pony poop attracts lots of flies. But I suppose no one said anything because I let all the neighborhood kids ride Midnight.

As an adult, I have gotten letters from some of these kids, now all grown up, with pictures of them astride my pony!

But maybe there were some complaints, because I remember we eventually found a real barn within walking distance of my house where we could board the pony. There were lots of other kids my age who had horses at "Moore's Barn," as it was called because it was owned by Old Man Moore and his ancient mother, who looked and acted like a witch.

We kids were scared to death of her.

Originally, I had a Western-style saddle to ride Midnight. My family would load Midnight up in a trailer on weekends and I would ride him in local horse shows. At the shows, I started noticing that the richer kids had their ponies decked out in English saddlery. In the South, like in Texas, horses always wore Western saddles. But to young Leslie, English saddles seemed fancier, even though they're less decorative and much more utilitarian. The way the leather is cut makes it easy to stay astride the horse but makes the saddle lighter so the horse can gallop over the countryside and any obstacles during fox hunts. English bridles also have a completely different bit, which is the piece the horse holds in his mouth, allowing you to steer him.

I ached for something different from my Western saddle. That year, I begged to get an English saddle and bridle for Christmas.

Well, Christmas morning came, and I got not only a new English saddle and bridle but also a new blanket to keep Midnight warm on chilly winter nights. If my uncle had not worked in a saddlery, I doubt my family could have afforded all that, but it made for the best Christmas since the one on which I'd gotten Midnight.

I also got a whole new set of English riding apparel. I

felt very fancy with my new duds. But when I look at pictures back then, Midnight appears a bit puzzled and out of place with all the fuss.

When I was young, I read every book ever written about horses or ponies.

I think the greatest gift my mother gave me was my love of reading. In the summertime, the bookmobile would pull into the elementary school parking lot once a week. At my mother's encouragement, I would walk down the hill and climb up into that lumbering bookmobile.

I loved everything about it.

First of all, it was air-conditioned, and Tennessee summers are brutal. I do not remember having air-conditioning in our home at that age. So to sit on the floor of the ice-cold bookmobile reading the selections I planned to check out that week was stupendous. Sometimes the bookmobile driver would have to run me off, as I would sit there all afternoon.

My favorite book about horses was *Misty of Chincoteague* by Marguerite Henry. It was a novel about the wild ponies of Chincoteague and Assateague islands off the

Maryland and Virginia shores. The herds of wild ponies who live on these islands are believed to have descended from the surviving horses of a Spanish galleon that wrecked off the coast in the 1500s.

On the last Thursday of July, the Chincoteague Volunteer Fire Department has the "Pony Penning," which draws thousands of visitors every year. There's a "pony swim," where they swim the herds to the mainland and auction off the foals.

It's been a lifelong dream of mine to attend the momentous event. Oddly enough, when I think about going there and watching the parade of ponies, I am alone. It's almost like I want to go back to my childhood memories of playing with pretend ponies in the solitude of our Tennessee backyard.

In my late twenties, I decided to try my hand at making a living working with horses. South of my hometown, about an hour above Atlanta, is a Thoroughbred horse breeding establishment named Old Mill Farm.

When I got there, I had no idea what was awaiting

me. The farm was one of many homes owned by Frances Weinman "Tippy" Luro. She was an heiress to a mining fortune left to her by her father.

My first day on the job, I was greeted by her daughter, Miss Cary Latimer Robinson, a well-known socialite in her own right. Cary was in her late forties at the time. She lived mainly in Miami and New York but would spent lots of time at the farm. Especially in the fall, when Georgia is beautiful with the colorful foliage.

Although it was midmorning, I believe Miss Latimer Robinson had already made a couple of trips to "the liquor closet," as they called the bar up in the big house. Bars are called that because they're often set up in a closet. You hear the term a lot around the Deep South.

Cary Latimer Robinson was incredibly beautiful. When she was young, she had been featured on the cover of *Collier's* magazine and was presented to society in New York at the 1954 Debutante Cotillion and Christmas Ball. She had also been on the cover of *Life* magazine in a riding habit with her saddlebred show horse.

She was a tiny bit weathered from years of trips to the liquor closet and smoking cigarettes but still lovely nonetheless.

Her son Billy Wright, who was and is a dear friend of

mine, once told me, "You can always tell when Mother's drinking. Her butt gets smaller and her hair gets higher."

Well, this particular morning, Miss Cary must have been on a roll. Her behind was ridiculously small and her hair was poofed sky-high. She had a cat under each arm and was holding two Bloomingdale's shopping sacks as she weaved her way down the shed row of the barn.

Not even bothering to ask who I was, she wailed, "Is Sammy around?"

Talk about a husky-sounding two-pack-a-day voice! She sounded like a sexy foghorn. I told her Sammy was off, as it was Sunday. "Is there anything I can do for you?"

"Well, darlin', as a matter of fact, there is. I'm beside myself this morning. These are Doolittle and Misty, my cats." She then began to whisper very dramatically, "They are inbred and highly nervous and must be swung daily. I'm just not up to it this morning."

"I beg your pardon?"

She plowed on, "Here, honey, I'll demonstrate. You put Doolittle down in this sack."

Meeeeow!

"Then you put Misty down in the other sack."

Meeeeow!

She began to perilously stagger in her chic slip-on

mule sandals up and down the barn hallway with the cats in the Bloomingdale's shopping sacks!

"Watch close, darlin'! You must do as I do. You must carry them with you while doing your chores around the barn. Swing them slowly. To and fro. To and fro. Ever so gently. Did I tell you they are inbred and highly nervous? And must be swung daily? They love being swung."

And with that, she handed me two cats ensconced in Bloomingdale's shopping sacks and headed back up to the big house.

I just stood there slack-jawed holding those darn cats. I carried them into the barn office and called Sammy. Before I could even get halfway through my story, he interrupted me.

"Damn that Cary. I tell you what, her clutch has been slipping for years. Take those cats and lock 'em in a stall. They'll be fine. When she comes back for 'em, tell her you swang 'em all morning."

And that's what I did.

When she came back for the cats, the first thing she asked was, "How long did you swing them? They still seem on edge."

I told her I swung them for an hour.

"Oh, darlin', that is not nearly enough. They'll be

climbing up the curtains. I won't be able to catch them. But if I can, I'll bring them down tomorrow morning for another session."

Fine, I thought. Tomorrow is my day off.

My job at Old Mill Farm was to help "break" the yearling racehorses to the saddle. This is a slow process; it takes months to get the "babies" ready for the racetrack.

You cannot very well just saddle them up, jump on and let them buck till they get used to it like you see in the Western movies.

These horses are worth millions of dollars. And, yes, they are coddled.

It all begins with lots of time spent with each horse in the safe surroundings of their stall. The young horses are rubbed and gently spoken to till they feel safe enough to have a saddle loosely strapped on their back. The saddle girth is tightened little by little over the next few days. Then a rider lies across the back of the horse to get the horse used to having weight on their back. After a few weeks of that, the rider throws all their weight on the back of the horse for the first time by mounting into the saddle.

HOW Y'ALL DOING?

This all happens in the stall.

After that, the horse is led up and down the barn hallway with the rider astride. Long "lead lines" are attached to the bit and pulled in each direction from behind, teaching the horse to go left and right upon demand.

Then the day arrives where the horse and rider are allowed to move about on their own.

Since I was so little and weighed just over a hundred pounds back then, I was usually the first one up. It was scary in the beginning, but I got really good at helping "break" the yearlings to saddle.

Mrs. Luro was married to one of the top trainers of all time: Horatio Luro. Luro came from Argentina in the late 1930s and made quite a success of himself in U.S. and Canadian horse racing, training many of the top racehorses.

At his peak, he won the 1962 Kentucky Derby with a horse named Decidedly and two years later won both the Derby and the Preakness with a horse called Northern Dancer. After Northern Dancer was retired from racing, he became an in-demand stud horse and sired many champions. His offspring have won every race imaginable.

The "Good Señor," as Luro was called, was eighty-three years old when I went to work for him. He still had all his marbles and was still riding his old horse all around the racetrack. In the fall, he would come down to the farm from New York to inspect the training of the yearlings. He ended up taking a real liking to me.

For some odd reason, he thought my deep Tennessee accent was an Irish one. He always called me "the Irish boy." Mrs. Luro would correct him constantly, telling him I was from Chattanooga, right above the farm, but he didn't listen.

The horses at Old Mill Road had to be shipped to most of their races. Shipping racehorses is an extremely exciting venture. The horses are blanketed, and their legs are wrapped in cotton, as the legs of a racehorse are the most important part of their anatomy and also easily subject to injury. Cotton batting is wrapped around all four legs and then held in place with stretchy tape. The horses are then led up long loading ramps onto huge semitrucks or sometimes even airplanes equipped with stalls that are filled with straw. Bags of hay are hung for the horses to munch on during the trip. They are cross-tied and not allowed to roam around the stalls while they are traveling.

When the yearlings were shipped to Hialeah Park's racetrack in Miami for the winter meet, Mr. Luro asked me to come along. I had only been working at the farm for less than a year, so I was beyond excited. He told me my job would be as "an exercise rider." I would get up incredibly early each morning and put the racehorses through their conditioning. At Mr. Luro's command, I would gallop around the track, increasing the speed and number of laps each day to get the horses ready to race.

I had harbored dreams of perhaps becoming a jockey who rode a horse in the race, but I very quickly found out I weighed too much. Each horse race is "handicapped" by the stewards of the track. A handicapper's dream would be for the race to end in a twelve-horse tie. They assign a weight to each horse according to the sex of the horse, the age of the horse, the number of races the horse has won and many other variables. Then they weigh the jockey and the saddle. The rest of the weight assigned is put into the saddle cloth with weighted bricks. Most jockeys keep their body weight at around a hundred and eight pounds.

Good Lord! I was a solid one hundred and twenty. I tried to lose the weight but couldn't. So I settled on being an exercise rider.

Back then, I owned a really cool 1973 MG convertible. I could pack everything I owned into that tiny car. It was as if I somehow knew that my life was headed toward a very nomadic period.

I followed close behind the horse vans in my sporty car as we caravanned along. Soon enough, it became my lifestyle. I would follow the horse vans to wherever the next racing meet was. After Hialeah Park, we headed north to

Belmont Park, outside of New York City, then up to Saratoga Springs for August and back to Belmont Park for the fall racing meet.

Then we shipped to Miami and it started all over again.

This was my life for many years, and I often look back on it as one of the happiest periods of my life.

But by the time I was in my early thirties, I was feeling the toll of constant traveling. I had been on the road then for eight or nine years. Eventually, I ended up back in Chattanooga looking for another way to seek my fortune. Something outside of the horse world.

I went back to school at the University of Tennessee at Chattanooga and enrolled in journalism classes. I was told that I needed to get all of my "electives" out of the way.

So I enrolled in Introduction to Theater. It was there I got the acting bug, which has sustained me for all these years. But my love of horses and my dream of owning a pony farm have never left me.

One day, a few years ago, I was driving out of the Warner Bros. studio and on a whim, I drove to the Los Angeles Equestrian Center, just to see what was going on. I had driven past many times, but I had never stopped in to take a look around.

It is seventy-five acres of horse paradise. There are barns devoted to every discipline within the horse world, from Western pleasure riding to hunter/jumpers and dressage. Each of the barns is rented out to a different trainer and owner. There's something for every horse enthusiast. I find it very fortuitous that the first barn I wandered into was the Jim Bennett stables, known for world-class saddlebred show horses.

I have always been fascinated with high-stepping show horses. It's a world eons away from the racehorse world I immersed myself in when I was younger. The American Saddlebred Horse Association was founded in Louisville, Kentucky, in 1891. It was the first organization for an American breed of horse. Saddlebreds are known for their high-stepping gaits. They walk, trot, slow rack, fast rack and canter. The slow rack and fast rack are what makes these horses desirable. Their gait is exceptionally smooth and easy on the rider.

And it is a purely American phenomenon to have these horses strutting around like peacocks in a show ring with judges.

I mistakenly thought that riding a horse was riding a horse. Even though I'd been on horseback from the time I was five or six years old, I had never taken a lesson. So, at sixty-five years of age, I decided to begin lessons in saddle seat equitation. The first thing you learn, as with any riding discipline, is the subtle nuances that figure into really good horsemanship.

It was the first time I had been on a horse in over thirty years, but it felt as if I were back on my old pony, Midnight.

I plan to continue my lessons until I can afford a show horse. Then I plan to buy a show horse. And I plan to ride my show horse at all the horse shows!

My dreams of a pony farm have grown to include room for saddlebred show horses. They will share the barns and paddocks with the wild ponies of Chincoteague.

And a good time is going to be had by all.

Aren't dreams the best!

I think our dreams are what sustain us in hard times. Dreams are what keep us childlike. I love that they can grow and expand as we grow and expand.

Since I've been "back in the barn," I've noticed I have had moments of unbridled happiness. I really do feel at times like young Leslie sitting astride a pony named Midnight decked out in the finest English saddlery.

THE MISSISSIPPI DELTA

It is said the Delta region of Mississippi will grab ahold of you and not let go. It is an alluvial plain, level land that has been created by large amounts of mineral-rich soil deposited by the mighty Mississippi River.

And right in the heart of the Delta is a town called Greenwood. It is the home of the Viking Range, which makes ovens that good cooks adore. Viking is headquartered on historic Cotton Row in downtown Greenwood. The company opened the Alluvian Hotel nearby as a tourist destination in 2003. The hotel has a spa, a cooking school and a wonderful restaurant, which gives this tiny Southern town a cosmopolitan feel.

And although I was not raised anywhere near the Delta, I must say, there is something about that part of the country that did grab ahold of me.

In my travels over the years, I have always tried to read books by authors from the area I am visiting. My job has afforded me the best experiences in travel. I am always visiting with a solid purpose, and on a per diem! Voraciously reading the local authors from where I'm working, I always get a wonderful sense of the local culture and history.

One hour west of Greenwood is a town called Greenville, Mississippi. The area around Greenville is fertile land where many Southern writers were born and bred. It is just brimming with literary history.

The best-known Mississippi writer, hands down, is William Faulkner. I am sure I would get no argument on that declaration. My relationship with Mr. Faulkner did not get off on the best footing. The first book I picked up of his was *The Sound and the Fury*. I sure wish I had known before I started that Benjy, the narrator of *The Sound and the Fury*, is intellectually disabled. If I had realized what Faulkner was up to, I might have read more of him from the get-go. But at the time, I was so frustrated trying to make heads or tails of what Benjy was wishing to convey, I threw the book across the room.

It took me years of reading to make my way back to Faulkner. And even though his writings seem to be one long extended sentence, I did thoroughly enjoy *As I Lay Dying*. I finally realized his brilliance.

And he certainly had the gift of encapsulating the South.

I initially had more luck with Eudora Welty, another well-known Mississippi author. Her writings about life in small Southern towns captured me from her first sentence. She, like me, was Southern to the bone.

Miss Welty seemed to be of the same writing school as Faulkner. Like him, she seemed to just run on and on. And nothing happened!

In her novel *Delta Wedding,* the family just meanders here and there getting ready for the oldest daughter's wedding. I was waiting for things to kick in! What was this all about?

But it all began to make sense when I tried to crack open *To the Lighthouse* by Virginia Woolf. She was a writer of the same generation as William Faulkner and Miss Welty. Virginia Woolf was certainly not a writer from anywhere near Mississippi, that's for sure. She was British born and a pioneer in the use of stream of consciousness as a narrative device.

It did not take long for me to realize why people would be afraid of Virginia Woolf.

But not me.

I am fearless when it comes to my reading. I will not let fancy-schmancy authors discourage me. I just look up various literary terms that critics have used when describing their novels. Words like "multiple focalization" and "lack of much dialogue and almost no action" and "written as thoughts and observations" jumped out at me with all three of these writers.

So, ready or not, Miss Eudora, here I come! I went back and reread Eudora Welty's *Delta Wedding* and loved it! Loved every single well-thought-out word of it.

When I read her short story "Why I Live at the P.O.," I laughed myself silly. Stella-Rondo and Uncle Rondo, in a "flesh-colored kimono cut on the bias," are characters that still make me giggle.

And then, when I was in college around 1975, I got to hear Miss Welty read "Why I Live at the P.O." aloud from a podium at the University of Tennessee.

You have not truly embraced Southern literature till you have heard it read aloud by the writer in an all-encompassing Southern accent.

As for current Southern writers, there is of course the prolific John Grisham, who was born in 1955, the same year as me. I think he is so handsome. He's over six feet tall, you know. And he just has that wonderful look of a well-mannered, well-brought-up Southern boy.

And when discussing Mississippi writers, let's not forget dear Julia Reed. I once had the chance to meet her and have lunch with her in New Orleans. It was a meal to be remembered. She originally hailed from Greenville, Mississippi. Unfortunately, she died in August of 2020. I was heartbroken when I heard about her unexpected death. She was still young and so talented. I had especially enjoyed her essays on the South in *Garden & Gun* magazine.

Not even a week after Julia's death, *Garden & Gun* approached me about being featured in their magazine. Although I wasn't sure how they knew, I assumed they wanted to talk about my brief friendship with Julia. Well, imagine my surprise when I found out it had nothing to do with Julia Reed or her death. It was just happenstance.

They interviewed me in depth about everything Southern under the sun and sent a photographer to my home to take a bunch of pictures. I wrote it all off as Miss Reed orchestrating it from above! We Southerners are raised to help one another and stick together through thick and thin.

In 2010, a magical thing brought me to the lush Delta region of Mississippi. I was cast in a movie filming in Greenwood called *The Help*. My part was small but fraught with meaning.

Not really. I made that up.

It was not fraught with meaning. It was just a tiny bit part. I played the newspaper editor who gives Emma Stone's character a job at the very beginning of the film.

I was well aware of *The Help* long before it went into production. I'm friends with Tate Taylor, who not only directed the film but wrote the screenplay and produced it. Almost ten years before, Tate and I had acted together in a popular stage show, Del Shores's *Southern Baptist Sissies*.

I am also friends with Brunson Green, one of *The Help*'s producers, and the actress Octavia Spencer, who won the Academy Award for Best Supporting Actress for playing Minny Jackson.

Tate grew up with the author Kathryn Stockett, who wrote the bestselling novel this wonderful movie was based on. I had heard all the stories. How they had known each other since preschool. How Tate had asked her to let him adapt the novel before it was even published. I heard about her perseverance when sixty agents rejected the manuscript, but the sixty-first accepted it.

HOW Y'ALL DOING?

I bet those sixty agents who rejected the script are kicking themselves, because *The Help* became a HUGE bestseller. Kathryn was approached by lots of big-time producers with checkbooks in hand who wanted to make it into a movie. But she stayed true to her word and allowed Tate to write the screenplay and direct even though he didn't have much experience. He had only directed and written one low-budget feature. Like I said, Southerners stick together.

Once the movie went into production, it acquired a cast to die for. At the first table read of the script after we all got to Mississippi, I was sitting next to Sissy Spacek. I could barely breathe. I had met her once before, as we were represented by the same manager for a while. But this seemed so up close and personal. I kept watching her out of the corner of my eye. She was scribbling in her script. On the other side of her was Viola Davis. She, too, was scribbling in her script. So, I thought I had better get to scribbling.

I pretended to scribble all kinds of things in my script.

Across the table from me were Octavia, Emma Stone, Bryce Dallas Howard, Allison Janney, Jessica Chastain, Anna Camp, Chris Lowell and many other wonderful actors too numerous to mention. I kept looking around for Cicely Tyson, as I'd heard she had been cast, but because of her advanced age, she came to Mississippi later on to shoot her scenes.

There was only one scene in the movie that involved the whole cast, the big Christmas party. We had to wear winter-appropriate black tie, tuxedos and long dresses, in that awful Mississippi heat. The scene was shot on the second floor of a big party venue, but they had to turn off the air conditioners when the camera was rolling, as they made too much noise.

It was so hot; we were all about to faint.

At one point, we were shooting a big master shot, where the camera panned across the dancing crowd of revelers. For some reason, when the camera turned my way, I impulsively performed a cartwheel. When the scene was over and they said cut, Tate Taylor asked me why I'd turned a somersault. It was not scripted.

I thought of a good one fast.

I told him, first of all, it was not a somersault, it was a cartwheel. Then I told him I was trying to lighten the mood, as everyone was grumpy from the heat. I said I'd thought turning a cartwheel for no reason would be cute.

He seemed unconvinced and told me my cartwheel would not be in the movie, period. I pouted about that for days. But being swept up in the jovial mood of shooting such a great movie, I soon forgot about my ill-fated acrobatics.

Imagine my surprise at the opening-night screening when I saw that my cartwheel had made the cut! There I was, big as life, on the movie screen, turning a cartwheel for no reason. It got a smattering of laughs from the audience. When I asked Tate what had made him decide to use my cartwheel in the final film, he told me it was not his decision. Stacey Snider, who was head of DreamWorks at the time, thought the movie could use some more comedy.

She thought my cartwheel was cute.

So there.

Most of my scenes in the movie were with Emma Stone. Tate had been singing her praises to the high heavens. He told me she was going to be the next Julia Roberts. When they trotted her out, all I saw was a gawky young girl.

At the time, I did not realize how much she had already gotten into her character, Eugenia "Skeeter" Phelan.

When we started shooting our scene, I could barely hear her. I'm used to loudmouths like Megan Mullally, who played Karen Walker on *Will & Grace*. I went over to tell Tate that she needed to pipe up. When I got to Tate, he was watching the scene we had just shot on the monitor. He seemed entranced with Emma's performance and was hardly paying attention to mine, so I used this opportunity to voice something that had been bothering me.

I said, "Tate, I'm not sure what I'm playing here."

"You are playing the newspaper editor," he said, looking at me like I was stupid.

"Well, I know that. But in the book, the newspaper editor seemed similar to the one in the *Superman* movies. He was loud and gruff. Should I be loud and gruff?"

Tate, bless his heart, took a moment to think.

This was long before I realized what a self-centered pain in the ass I am sometimes. The scene we were shooting was one of the very first scenes in the movie. It was about introducing Emma's character, Skeeter, to the audience. She was the lead in the movie, and it was especially important at this point in the film to see what she was all about. The scene was not about me. My character was there to serve the film and Skeeter's journey.

But Tate took a moment. "Leslie, here's the way I see your character. Every Southern town has one."

"One what?" I was truly perplexed.

"That man who is married with five children, but everybody 'knows.'"

HOW Y'ALL DOING?

"Knows what?" I asked. Tate looked at me like I should know. He turned away and began to deal with another problem.

And then it hit me.

The town sissy.

That's what I was playing. The town sissy.

Well, I thought, that shouldn't be a stretch.

I finished all my scenes with Emma, and I was still on the fence about whether she was really the next Julia Roberts. But I must say I had a huge epiphany when I saw her work on the big screen. There were a million things happening in her face and voice I had not noticed, even though I had been sitting only a few feet from her. I was so wrapped up in the business of trying to figure out who my character was supposed to be and what a newspaper editor should be doing, I had not noticed that Emma Stone is an incredibly gifted actress. I feel honored to have worked with her.

I have so many wonderful memories of shooting that movie in Greenwood. You might think most of my memories would involve getting to work with all those big movie stars. Sure, some of them are, but not all of them.

One of my best memories from Greenwood involves a puppy. A few famous actors were a part of this memory, but the puppy was the real star.

When I first arrived in the Jackson, Mississippi, airport, I had been told the film's transportation department would pick me up and drive me two hours to Greenwood. Upon landing, I walked around the baggage claim area looking for someone with a sign and encountered Allison Janney. She told me she thought they must have forgotten to send someone to get us.

Forgotten?

Lord have mercy, I could see them forgetting me, but ALLISON JANNEY? She was a big star! She made some calls and indeed, they had gotten our flights mixed up. Now no one could come get us. Allison, being the easygoing soul she is, was unfazed. She told them not to worry, she would rent a car and drive the two hours from Jackson to Greenwood.

As we were exiting the airport, we encountered two other actors from the movie, Wes Chatham and Tiffany Brouwer.

"They ain't coming to get us. Follow me," I instructed.

I mainly said it because Wes Chatham was so damn good-looking. And Tiffany was real pretty, too. But mainly because Wes Chatham was so damn good-looking.

HOW Y'ALL DOING?

"So, I guess I'm renting a minivan," mumbled Allison under her breath.

"Hush. He's cute," I said. "They will pay you back from petty cash."

Soon enough, off we went with Allison at the wheel. The drive was lovely until we spotted something profoundly disturbing. Cowering in the middle of the two-lane highway was a puppy! Allison quickly slammed on the brakes, just missing the poor thing. When the car was stopped, we jumped out and approached the puppy. He was in the tall grass by the side of the road, scared out of his wits.

My heart broke.

I suppose someone had tossed the puppy out of the car, since we were in the middle of nowhere, too far out for a puppy to get to on her own. Who on earth would do such a thing? People like that need to burn in hell, I'll tell you that much.

It was a beautiful puppy. Real big. It looked almost like an Irish setter. But it seemed hungry and very frightened. There on the side of the road, we cooed and stroked it till it calmed down. Then we loaded it in the car. I held it in my lap as we drove straight to the set.

Although none of us had to work that day, the production was already in full swing. When we got out of the car with our newfound charge, everyone gathered around us.

We had already decided to name the pup Skeeter, after Emma Stone's character. But that was about all we had decided.

What on earth were we going to do with this puppy?

Well, Bryce Dallas Howard took one look at that poor creature and took charge. She's a take-charge kind of gal, and thank goodness for that. The rest of us were so befuddled about what to do next. Right away, Bryce located a local vet that could take the puppy the next day to give it a good examination and shots.

I came up with the idea of passing a bucket around the set, asking for donations to help us. It was the perfect job for me as I was used to passing the plate on Sunday morning at the Baptist church.

There is a real art in learning how to give a beseeching look as the plate is passed. It makes folks open up their pocketbooks. We hit pay dirt, as the whole cast and crew had gotten their per diem that day and everyone had cash.

I think I collected almost four hundred dollars.

Since Skeeter could not go to the vet till the next day and she needed somewhere to go, she somehow ended up at Tate Taylor's rented house for the night. There was a big commotion since Tate's dog did not like the intruder. I also heard Skeeter tried to get into a kitchen garbage pail, got the lid stuck on her head and went berserk, running all around the house in the middle of the night, waking everyone up.

By the next morning, we quickly realized Skeeter seemed to be saddled with some rather alarming behavioral problems. Most likely on account of her sketchy youth. If truth be told, that dog was a nervous wreck. We doubted we would ever find her a forever home. She was a certified nut job. I was scared to death that if we gave her away, Skeeter might end up at the local dog pound, or worse.

But all is well that ends well.

The money left over from the bucket I had passed around was used to hire a trainer to work with dear Skeeter. She responded beautifully to her instructions and passed all her tests with flying colors. With Bryce Dallas Howard leading the charge, we found a forever home with an understanding family in Greenwood for our wayward Skeeter.

A job well done!

At the end of our time in Greenwood, after the movie wrapped, we all agreed that we had to keep up with one another once we got back to Los Angeles. But I'd been around enough movie sets to know that would not happen.

It never does. Life goes on and we get back to our usual routines. I have not hung out with a single person from *The Help* since the premiere, but the precious memories linger. That's enough for me.

All I remember of the premiere is how beautiful Jessica Chastain looked. You know, some girls are just made for the red carpet, and she's one of them.

Early the next year, she and Octavia were nominated for Academy Awards for their roles in *The Help*. That was so thrilling! In all my years in the business, I had never known anyone who was nominated for such a prestigious award, much less won one!

The night of the Oscars, I was home in my pajamas watching the festivities on television. When Octavia won, I was so overcome I dialed her number so I could be one of hundreds who were filling her voicemail with messages of congratulations.

Imagine my surprise when she answered. She had just walked offstage! "What do you want, baby?"

I jumped into an explanation. "I really did not expect you to answer, honey. I was just so overjoyed and proud. I couldn't contain myself. And you look so pretty. That white Grecian gown is amazing."

HOW Y'ALL DOING?

Octavia laughed out loud. "Double Spanxed, baby. I am doubled Spanxed. And I can barely breathe."

Hilarious! That is just hilarious!

The Mississippi Delta always seems to jump into my consciousness from the oddest places. I recently did a film for the director Lee Daniels. It is called *The United States vs. Billie Holiday.* Mr. Daniels had already finished the film, but he felt it still needed a few scenes. With the agreement of Paramount, he was given one day to do some reshoots.

There was one area in the film Lee felt needed a little more exploring. He came up with the rather ingenious idea of having Billie Holiday be interviewed near the end of her life in 1959.

He wanted an insipidly clueless gossip columnist of that era who would have the audacity to ask stupid questions like, "Tell me, honey, what is it really like to be a colored woman?"

Billie Holiday's story was so tragic. She became addicted to heroin, and no matter how hard she tried, she was never able to completely kick the dangerous addiction. The U.S. government tried to use her personal struggles against her to keep her from singing her powerful song "Strange Fruit," which had been written by a teacher in response to the lynchings of Thomas Shipp and Abram Smith in Indiana. When Lee called to offer me the part he had written with me in mind, he asked me if I had ever heard of Skip E. Lowe. He wanted the character to be an amalgam of Skip E. Lowe and Quentin Crisp.

"Oh Lord, Lee, I have been told I resemble Skip E. Lowe since I got to Hollywood. And as you know, that is not a compliment."

But we really did look somewhat alike.

Skip E. Lowe was a D-list celebrity who acted like he was on the A-list. I suppose you could call him a gossip columnist. He had been something of a child star and had written a book called *The Boy with the Betty Grable Legs*. I thought the whole thing was creepy.

Mr. Lowe had one of the first cable-access talk shows. This was back when cable access was populated by shows such as *The Robin Byrd Show*, which I watched religiously for the male nudity. She had male strippers dance around completely nude. You could see their peckers and everything else. Robin Byrd was a former pornography actress who would dance all around in a crocheted bikini singing her theme song, "Baby Let Me Bang Your Box."

HOW Y'ALL DOING?

In the early days of cable access, just about anything was allowed.

On his show, Mr. Lowe would have campy guests such as Mamie Van Doren, and they would sit, drink and gossip. Skip would get smashed. He was a momentous drunk. I used to see Mr. Lowe parading around Hollywood like a D-list Truman Capote. He wore hats and flowing scarves and flounced all around—snappily dressed, but if you looked closely, you realized the clothes were from the thrift store instead of a designer boutique.

So, when Lee Daniels told me he wanted me to resemble Skip E. Lowe, I did a little bit of research. As I was reading about him, one thing jumped out at me.

Skip E. Lowe was from Greenville, Mississippi.

Well, of course he was. It just made sense.

Why this little town keeps popping up in my life is a mystery to me. But I suppose we should hoist one for Greenville, Mississippi.

A place that grabbed ahold of me and has not let go.

THE BRIDE DOLL

I have always loved and had a deep fascination with dolls. When I was a child, there was so much shame attached to a boy's liking them. I also cherished Easy-Bake Ovens, but don't get me started on how that was received.

A few years ago, people fearfully thought if a little boy wanted to play with dolls, he might turn out queer.

Well, I did.

Play with dolls and turn out queer, I mean.

Being queer is such an integral part of who I am and why I am who I am. I can't imagine myself any other way.

And I don't want to be any other way. And I certainly don't think playing with dolls is why I'm gay.

I'm sure there are many little boys who played with dolls and are not gay. Hopefully by now, we have progressed to the point where fearing a child might be queer is way down the list of parental fears.

I was always an odd child. I kept up with all the goings-on outside my suburban upbringing. I read gossip magazines and always knew which movie star was going with which movie star. I followed the way they all dressed and the way the women wore their hair. When Mia Farrow cut off all her hair, I almost fainted. She had married Frank Sinatra and it was all over the news. That pixie cut fascinated me.

There was also a model out of London named Twiggy. I don't know how on earth I learned about her, but I did. Her haircut was iconic, and she wore false eyelashes on the top of her eyelids and on the bottom, which gave her big, beautiful eyes.

I remember my sisters got a Tressy doll. You could push a button on Tressy's stomach and her hair would grow. I kid you not. She had a long ponytail that stuck out of the top of her head and when you pressed that button, the ponytail got longer and longer. I wanted to get my hands on that doll so bad. I did not want to play with her or dress her up. No, I had constructed some big plans for Tressy.

One day, in a fit of inspiration, I took a pair of scissors to the Tressy doll. I cut off her long, flowing ponytail and cropped her hair into a stylish pixie cut. Then I took a black ink pen and gave her Twiggy lashes.

It did not turn out as I expected.

She looked god-awful and real scary. Shorn of all her hair, with black circles around her eyes, she looked like a drug-crazed mental patient.

I knew I was in big trouble.

In a panic, I threw Tressy out the window into the yard. Every day or so, I would go out there and check on her. I've seen murderers do that on my murder programs. They are always checking on the body and that's how they get caught.

Poor Tressy. It had rained and the ink had run down her face, making her look even more deranged than before. She looked like she belonged in a Salvador Dalí painting.

She was a terrifying sight.

When one of my twin sisters finally came upon Tressy, you've never heard such caterwauling. I had known Tressy would eventually be found, but I was not prepared for the hubbub it caused.

Boy, I got it. I really got it.

Around this same time, there was a family in my neighborhood who seemed fancy to me. We were just a middle-class suburb and I doubt this family had more money than us. But for some reason, they just seemed kinda fancy.

The family had a girl around my age. She always wore the cutest clothes to school. Her outfits were always the height of fashion. The rumor was the family took shopping trips to Atlanta.

My goodness! Shopping trips to Atlanta!

Since we were close in age, I was invited over to play occasionally. But it all seemed so formal to me. It was the first time I ever heard that little boys should not be allowed in little girls' bedrooms. That did not make sense to me. I had run in and out of my sisters' bedroom my whole life. Not to mention all my girl cousins' bedrooms.

But at this house, I was told that I must not go in this fancy girl's bedroom by her father. I also noticed a look on his face when he looked at me. I had seen this same look on my own daddy's face.

It was not a look of pity.

It was not a look of anger.

It was more of a quizzical look. It was as if they could not figure me out.

HOW Y'ALL DOING?

I was not the butchest little boy to come down the pike, that's for sure. But I was a joyful child. I was fun to be around. And I had learned to be really funny. I learned to be funny to keep the bullies at bay. But apparently, most little boys did not act the way I acted. At least that was what I read in their faces when grown men gave me the once-over.

When I was invited over to the fancy family's house, it seemed highly organized. It felt like what they now call a "playdate."

A playdate?

The rest of us kids just ran wild. We ran all over the neighborhood. Especially in the summertime. We were out the door after breakfast and didn't come home till the streetlights began to beam at night. Most of the time, we ran in and out of people's houses without even knocking.

We never paid attention to the adults.

Except, I do remember one family who were kinda trashy with a million kids. Their daddy would walk around in his underpants holding a beer. And his underpants were not boxers, like my daddy wore; they were tight white Fruit of the Looms that he pulled up past his belly button.

I thought it was very comical.

When I was invited over to this little girl's house and got a gander at her Barbie doll collection, I couldn't believe my eyes. She kept all her dolls in a romper room, so I was allowed in. She had every outfit that Mattel ever put out for the Barbie doll. And they were all displayed beautifully on tiny stands. She had the *Roman Holiday* outfit, the Nighty Negligee set, Plantation Belle's outfit and my personal favorite, Evening Splendor, which was a black evening dress with a little fake-fur hat and fake-fur cuffs.

I coveted the Cotton Casual outfit, which was a strapless navy-and-white-striped dress with a dirndl skirt. It had a red bow at the bodice with little red slip-on Barbie doll kitten heels.

She also had all the groovy sixties outfits. My favorite was a wild and wacky neon-pink fake-fur jacket with a tiny denim miniskirt and white go-go boots.

Those boots were made for walking, I'll tell you that much.

She also had Sweater Girl, who seemed like Barbie from an earlier era. It was back when girls did exercises for their busts. I saw it on television in a comedy skit. All these busty girls were in a line giggling and doing bust exercises.

"We must, we must, we must increase our bust. The

bigger, the better we look in a sweater. We must increase our bust."

One of her dolls even had the Apple Print Sheath.

The sheath was the rage. It was what all the ladies were wearing back then, simple cotton sheaths with bright, vibrant prints. I asked my grandmother Griffin, who was my mother's mother, if she would teach me how to sew an apple-print sheath for a doll.

She readily agreed.

She was always sewing. She had raised seven kids without a lot of money. She certainly knew her way around a McCall's pattern. We dug in her drawers and found fabric scraps. We couldn't find any with an apple print, but she did have other fabrics with fruit prints. She let me pick out the fabric and we sewed a doll sheath. I was so proud of that little dress.

It's odd; I remember sewing it, but I don't remember showing it to anyone. I suppose I knew I was supposed to be ashamed of sewing a dress for a doll. I think I left the sheath in a drawer at my grandmother's house.

I always think about how remarkable my grandmother was. She never, in any way, questioned why a little boy like me wanted to sew a dress for a doll. When I told my mother I was gay, one of her concerns was that she did not want her mother and daddy to know. They were old and she felt they would not understand. I found out years later from a cousin that my grandmama and granddaddy had suspected I was gay since I was two years old. And they loved me all the more for it.

Having had seven children, they were blessed with lots of grandchildren. But I think I was their favorite.

Around the time I was doing the movie *The Help*, my fellow actor Viola Davis adopted a baby girl. One of the producers for *The Help* gave her a baby shower and I was invited. I had never been to a baby shower in my life. I knew you were supposed to bring a present. But what?

I had no idea. Perhaps a baby doll? I walked over to the mall and there it stood in all its glory. The American Girl store. I walked in and all of it came flooding back, my love of dolls and doll clothes. I realized I could spend hours in that store.

And remarkably, I did not feel one ounce of shame for loving everything in that store. I suppose it was the work I had done in my recovery programs about ridding myself of shame.

No shame in my game.

HOW Y'ALL DOING?

But it was a long road to letting go of that.

My spiritual advisor who worked with me in the early days of my recovery was a man named Don Norman. He died recently and I miss him daily. He was a saucy African American gay man who made me laugh out loud constantly but always kept me in my place. He couldn't have cared less that I had once guest-starred on *Murphy Brown*.

Oh my, he could get you told.

Most people think recovery is about quitting all the alcohol and substances. Well, that is the hard part. But recovery is really about learning to live, one day at a time, without the use of anything that affects us from the neck up.

To be happy and content.

I had seen Don Norman around the rooms of recovery for years and loved the way he "walked the walk." He was not one of those people who could only talk a good game. So when I had three years clean and sober, I asked him if he would work with me and help me.

His answer was immediate and finite.

"Oh, no, no, no, honey. I can't work with you. Too much drama, honey. You're always wrapped up in the drama."

I can honestly say I had not one idea what he was talking about.

Surprisingly, I was not miffed about his response. I just moved on and asked others to work with me. Then when I was five years sober, I hit a wall. I realized most of my problems stemmed from my own internal homophobia. I had fallen out of the womb into my mother's high heels and been ashamed my whole life.

I was once told that I was a "fag-hating fag." It's an awful way to put it, but it seemed to sum up that horrible feeling.

This shame was keeping me from the Sunlight of the Spirit. That's a recovery idea. When you live in the Sunlight of the Spirit, you live a life free of resentments.

I cornered Don Norman at a meeting and poured out my soul. Without hesitation, he said, "We are gonna start with a fear list. Call me at ten minutes after eight in the morning and tell me four of your fears. Remember to call me at ten minutes after eight. Not a minute before and not a minute after. I got lots of folks I am working with."

Good Lord. He was so bossy.

But I dialed him up the next morning promptly at ten minutes after eight. He answered on the first ring. "What you 'fraid of, baby?"

"Um . . . heterosexual men. Um . . . getting sick with

AIDS . . . and um . . . that I sound like a big sissy when I talk . . . and um . . . heights."

He giggled, "Oooooh, gurl, I don't know how you leave the house with all them fears! Call me in the morning at ten minutes after eight and list four more fears. Plus, go to a meeting today and welcome every single newcomer. Give 'em a handshake and look 'em right in the eye, baby."

Click.

Good Lord.

This went on for months. I got up to eighty fears on my list. I constantly complained that I had no idea how this was going to rid me of my shame. But he wouldn't listen. All he would tell me was that all my problems were fear based.

He was right.

My next assignment involved taking each fear and listing whether it was "real" or "imagined." I was a little perplexed. He explained, "If a bear is chasing you in the woods, baby, that's a real fear. That bear might eat you. But most of our fears are just imagined."

Not most for me. All of my fears were imagined. Don Norman also had me write how I thought I had acquired each fear. I wrote for days and days, years and years.

Slowly, I began to realize how much my imagined fears

and how much my shame had hindered me throughout my life. Since then, I have tried to live a fearless and shame-free life in the Sunlight of the Spirit, just as Don taught me.

So when I walked into the American Girl store and felt no shame at my love of dolls, it was a milestone moment. Not one with trumpets blaring and angels singing, but a nice quiet realization that I had changed.

I had such a hard time picking a doll for the baby. One of the great things about the American Girl brand is their line of Truly Me dolls. A young girl or boy, as they have both, can pick a doll with the same eye, hair and skin color. But as I wandered the store, I saw a doll that was dressed up in a horseback-riding outfit.

What a quandary! What a choice!

Eventually, I settled on the horseback-riding doll and called it a day. At the shower, all the girls got a good giggle at my choice. It would be years before Viola's baby would be old enough to play with that doll. But I figured she could place it in the nursery, and it would be sitting ready whenever the baby got old enough. Maybe it wasn't a traditional gift for a shower, but I bet you money that little girl will love her horseback-riding doll. I know I do. I saw her in the window of the American Girl store recently and she looked great.

HOW Y'ALL DOING?

There is a story my family often tells about me and the bride doll.

When I was three, my daddy wanted to take me to a wedding. My mother was a little hesitant. "You know, Allen, he is an excitable boy. I am worried he won't sit still in the pew during the ceremony."

But Daddy was adamant. "Well, Peggy, it is my army buddy getting married and I want to show my boy off. So, can we figure this out?"

It started off as the disaster my mother feared.

As soon as we sat down, they could not keep me still in the pew. I was up. I was down. I chattered incessantly, asking all kinds of questions. Mother finally, in desperation, told Daddy she was going to take me outside so I would not disrupt the ceremony.

But at that very moment, the organ swelled, everyone stood and the bride swept down the aisle. Mother said I froze like a pointer dog. I stood stock-still, with my eyes glued to the bride, as she floated by in a cloud of white tulle.

I remember its being the most thrilling pageantry I had witnessed in my three years on earth. I was breathless. Afterward, it was all I could talk about for days. In celebration of it all, I made up a game called Bright and Goon, my three-year-old way of saying "Bride and Groom."

I was the Bright.

I put an angel food cake pan on my head and slipped my mother's white terry-cloth bathrobe on backward for my bridal gown. It was off-the-shoulder and Empire waisted, and I was a vision of loveliness. I made my poor female cousin be the Goon and walk me all around the house.

That Christmas, when they took me to Loveman's department store to sit on Santa Claus's lap, I proudly announced I wanted Santa Claus to bring me . . . a bride doll!

My daddy was not too happy with my choice. "I am not getting him a bride doll, Peggy."

Mother told him not to worry. "You know how he is, Allen. If we do not mention it again, maybe he will forget about it."

This was not to be the case. No, ma'am. No, no, no. No siree, Bob.

Christmas Eve, it was all I talked about. "Santy Claus is going to bring me a bride doll. And I am going to play wedding and brush her hair."

My childish enthusiasm must have really affected my mother. She went to Daddy in tears. "Allen, are you going

HOW Y'ALL DOING?

to explain it to him in the morning when there is no doll under the tree? I will not know what to say."

Still upset, she went into the kitchen to start cooking the Christmas feast. In a few minutes, she heard the front door shut.

Now, please bear in mind, in 1958, my career-army daddy scoured Chattanooga, Tennessee, in a freak snowstorm, to find his beloved three-year-old son a bride doll.

Okay, full disclosure. I made up the snowstorm. I have no idea why I felt the need to add a snowstorm to embellish this story when the story is a big deal on its own! A man's man like my daddy hitting the toy stores looking for a bride doll for his son in 1958! No snowstorm needed.

The next morning, I flew into the living room and there she was, under the Christmas tree. My bride doll! She was LIFE-SIZED to a three-year-old and stared at me out of a cellophane wrapper. She had a long white dress, white pearls and a lace veil!

I squatted on the floor and peed all over the place.

Thank you, Daddy. For having enough love for your son to buy him a doll.

And thank you, Don Norman. For helping me live a joyful, shame-free life.

I hope the two of you have met in the sweet by-and-by.

MY LAST FIRST PITCH

When I was asked to be the grand marshal for the Capital Pride Parade in 2016, I was really jazzed. I have done many Gay Pride festivals over the years and even had the honor of being the grand marshal at a few. But this Pride was taking place in our nation's capital, and it seemed like a big deal.

When they called me in California to settle the particulars, they told me I would be featured in a parade riding in a convertible. I came up with a better idea.

"How about instead of riding in a convertible, I ride a tiny pony down the parade route? Wouldn't that be hilarious?"

They seemed a little hesitant, as if this were not possible. But I loved my idea! And in my helter-skelter impulsive way, I decided to move ahead with or without their blessings.

I didn't have to worry about the pony part. When I was a kid, ponies were a hot commodity. After all my years of riding, I felt confident I could ride a pony down the parade route. Knowing I was up for the challenge and that my plan was sure to be a riot, I decided to deal with first things first. I wanted new riding clothes, so I went to the Los Angeles Equestrian Center and bought a full riding outfit. I had stylish jodhpurs, shiny knee-high riding boots, a tweed hunting jacket and a velvet riding cap.

That stuff is not cheap, but I looked terrific in it.

I packed it carefully and took off on a cross-country flight for Capital Pride. The next day, I got ready at my hotel and arrived for the parade fully trussed in my new outfit. I thought I was going to faint in the June heat of DC, but I soldiered on.

HOW Y'ALL DOING?

Except there was no pony.

When I asked where the pony was, they were extremely apologetic. "Oh, Mr. Jordan, we thought you were kidding."

"Does it look like I'm kidding?" I motioned from my head to my toes at my glamorous riding habit.

Well, this was a fine how-do-you-do!

I was going to look like a fool riding in a convertible in my horse-riding outfit. But I was not about to go back to the hotel and change. I saw a Kinko's across the street and I quickly came up with an idea. I walked over and asked them if I could get a sign made in a rush.

An hour later, I jumped into the convertible and off we went, with me dressed in my riding finery holding a big sign.

BUT I WAS PROMISED A PONY!

It was evident early on from the puzzled looks of the Pride participants along the parade route that few understood what was going on with me and my sign. But I sure had fun, and my enthusiasm had an effect on the crowds. The parade that day was a spectacular display of pride and showmanship.

But that night, tragedy struck.

Down in Orlando, Florida, an armed man walked into a gay nightclub called the Pulse and opened fire. Forty-nine people were killed and fifty-three were wounded.

Among those dead was the young man who opened fire. We all woke to the disastrous news.

At the time, it was the largest mass shooting on U.S. soil.

I was struck to my core by this news. There was the anger that welled knowing my people had been targeted. I have performed in the Orlando area for years and I have many friends there. Gay friends. Gay friends that like to go out to bars.

It did not take long for my phone to begin ringing. I learned the jewelry designer who had made some fabulous costume jewelry for my character Brother Boy in the movie I did called *A Very Sordid Wedding* had died.

There were several more I knew among the dead.

It also solidified an idea I'd had in my head for years. I began going to gay bars as a teenager. Since I am barely five feet tall, I have always suffered minor incidents of claustrophobia in gay bars. The way people are crammed in has always struck me as an accident waiting to happen. And the noise is immense. With the disco speakers thumping, no one could possibly hear a cry for help.

On that dreadful morning, I was taken to the White House. This in and of itself was momentous. I wish, in retrospect, my trip to the White House had been under different circumstances.

HOW Y'ALL DOING?

But it was what it was.

There had been a bevy of activity from the Pride committee, as this monstrous happening had pulled all the planned events asunder. The Washington Gay Men's Chorus was already on board to greet the tour line of folks visiting the White House as part of Pride Week. I was asked along with my friend Ty Herndon, an openly gay country music recording artist, to come to the White House as well, all at the invitation of President and First Lady Obama.

Ty and the chorus had also been asked before the Orlando massacre to sing the national anthem at a Washington Nationals game the following Tuesday, as part of the Pride celebrations. They were using this time in the White House to practice. With all the tragedy that had unfolded, it gave added weight to this appearance.

As the chorus sang "God Bless America," I was approached by one of the committee members. "Mr. Jordan, don't forget you've agreed to throw the first pitch out at the game on Tuesday."

Oh yeah.

That.

Well, there was one small problem I needed to deal with. I had never thrown a baseball in my life. I had held a baseball, but I had never once thrown a baseball. The thought of standing on the pitcher's mound at a major league baseball game scared the bejesus out of me.

What on earth had I gotten myself into?

There was much more at stake than my making a fool of myself. Oh, trust me, it was bigger and went deeper than that. When I was about six or seven, my daddy signed me up for T-ball and I was hopeless. They put me way out in the outfield. It was so hot and boring out there. To pass the time, I would practice cheerleader jumps the neighbor girl across the street had taught me.

My poor dad would holler, "Don't do that! Don't do those jumps!"

So, I just lay down and put the mitt over my face. I lay real still and pretended I was dead like a possum. I think my dad realized I was miserable, and he certainly did not want that. So I was relieved of my duties.

No more T-ball, thank goodness.

Mother told me that when she was in labor with me, my daddy was going room to room, up and down the hospital halls, introducing himself to everybody and telling all who would listen that his wife was about to have "a boy."

Back then, you did not know the sex of a child until it was born, but Mother said Daddy was convinced. And sure enough, once I arrived, I was a boy. He ran back down the hall making the announcement that "his boy" had arrived.

My daddy used to take me everywhere with him. He was extremely outgoing and friendly. He loved to introduce himself to perfect strangers. We'd be in the line at the grocery store, and he would strike up a conversation with others in the queue.

"Hello, I'm Allen Jordan and this is my boy, Leslie." I would give a little wave and smile, but on the inside I was mortified.

"Oh, Dad . . ."

Or we'd be at a stoplight and he'd strike up a conversation with the next car. "Hey, buddy, what year is that car? Is that a 1961?"

I would lie down on the floorboard.

When my dad's plane went down, I was eleven. That is a terrible time for a boy to lose his father. Especially a little boy who fell out of the womb and landed in his mama's high heels. From the day of his funeral on, I was haunted by the feeling that perhaps I had been a disappointment to my daddy. He was such a sports fanatic and I had failed at T-ball.

That belief in his disappointment was my secret shame, one I carried into adulthood.

Why is it that we love to drag all that baggage from

childhood with us? We heave it dutifully. We haul it everywhere we go. And we pull it out at the drop of a hat for all to see. Nope, we are not going to let go of all that baggage.

Not me, at least. And from the plethora of self-help books on the matter, I do not think I am alone.

I asked my mother once if she felt Dad had been ashamed of me. You would have thought I'd slapped her. She was flabbergasted. "What on earth would give you that idea? Your daddy ADORED you, Leslie. The sun rose and set with you."

I knew that, but I pressed my mother to please try to remember if he'd ever mentioned my not being good at sports. I told her it was important for me to know.

She pondered for a minute. "I do remember him asking me once why you only played with girls. And I told him, I said, 'Allen, there are not that many boys in the neighborhood his age for him to play with.'"

That was the summer they decided to send me to camp at the Baylor School. It was exhausting. So many activities I had no interest in.

Archery? No thank you.

Dodgeball? No thank you.

Nature hikes? No thank you.

A big bonfire and wiener roast? Must I?

HOW Y'ALL DOING?

My only big interest at that age was horses and ponies. I had my own pony, Midnight, whom I missed during camp days. I just wanted to be riding Midnight. But the camp was situated on the campus of the Baylor School. Back then it was just for boys but now it is a school for boys and girls.

At the conclusion of the camp we had Parents' Day. All the parents gathered on the bleachers of the ball field and ribbons were passed out. They announced the ribbon for the best in archery. They gave out a ribbon for the best swimmer. This was followed by a ribbon for the best in track and field.

I didn't win anything.

My dad sunk lower and lower in his seat, thinking he might have scarred me for life. But then one of the counselors brought out a trophy. "And now, we would like to present a trophy for best all-around camper. This little guy was not always the best at what he attempted, but he sure kept us laughing. Come on up here, Leslie Jordan!"

Honey, I won a trophy. No tacky little ribbon for this boy. My dad was jumping up and down. He was so proud.

But here is the kicker: I do not remember much about the camp or the trophy. But I can remember my failure at T-ball like it was yesterday. The thing about shame is that it is so selective. I knew my dad loved me. He showed it daily in a million different ways. So why remember failures?

The day before the dreaded first pitch, I was appearing on Fox 5, a Washington, DC, morning staple. My interviewer was Wisdom Martin. I loved his name and told him so. We talked a little about the origin. His father was named Wisdom and he named one of his kids Wisdom.

Little did I know that his "wisdom" was going to save the day!

During the interview, I told Wisdom about my fear of throwing the first pitch out when I had never thrown a baseball in my life. When the interview was over, he told me that he coached Little League and if I wanted, he could teach me to pitch.

I was ecstatic.

Off we traipsed to the parking lot of the TV station and Wisdom gave me some unbelievably valuable tips about throwing a baseball from the pitcher's mound. When I left, I had a working knowledge of what was expected, I had practiced my pitch and I felt much better about the coming ordeal.

At the very least, I was not going to make a total fool of myself.

HOW Y'ALL DOING?

For folks who have trouble finding and believing in a "Higher Power," as we sometimes refer to God in the rooms of recovery, I would like to submit a thought. In each of our lives, there are extraordinary happenings that could easily be chalked up to serendipity. But I personally choose to believe that on the Tuesday evening at the Nationals' stadium when Leslie Allen Jordan was called upon to throw out the first pitch, he did so bathed in a godly light, some sort of heavenly illumination.

The Washington Gay Men's Chorus had finished and Ty Herndon had wrapped up a sterling rendition of "The Star-Spangled Banner" when my name was announced.

I ran out to the pitcher's mound with a baseball in hand.

I silently prayed, Dear God, please help this pitch be in loving memory of my forty-nine murdered comrades, and I suppose I must pray for the soul of the young man who committed this heinous crime. So please let this pitch be in memory of the fifty who died. But most of all, I would like for this pitch to be in memory of my daddy, Major Allen Bernard Jordan, who gave his life in service to his country.

I ran to the pitcher's mound very carefully, trying not to look so athletically challenged. I stood tall and hurled that ball with all my might. I hurled it so hard, I fell down.

I am not sure if it made it to home plate or not. But there was a roar from the crowd and the catcher came out to congratulate me.

Through all of this major hubbub, I keenly felt the presence of my dad. He was such a loving and kind man. I knew he would have been so proud. There was something lifted from my shoulders.

The pitcher even presented me with the ball as a keepsake.

Over the years, I have told this story a million times as part of my one-man show. And for reasons unknown, I have wildly embellished.

Honey, if embellishment were a sin, I would be sitting in a roaring fire with Beelzebub right now.

You would have thought I had learned my lesson years earlier after the fiasco I created when I embellished a story about a woman in my church. She had a baby, out of wedlock, who resembled a baby pig. Well, by the time I was done telling the story, that woman not only had a baby that looked like a pig, she'd also been shot in the church parking lot by some boys who were "slashing good Christian people's tires!"

I cannot remember how it all started, but I am fairly sure that the woman who had the baby did not get shot in the church parking lot after she admonished some boys who were "slashing good Christian people's tires!"

Where on earth would I even get the idea for this story?

I told that story so many times that Linda Bloodworth-Thomason picked it up as a story line on a series I did years ago called *Hearts Afire*. Then I really had to embellish to keep the story alive both in the press and on the show.

The same thing happened with my tale of the first pitch. The story grew bigger and bigger. It took on a life of its own. It was as if I could not help myself.

I added a hernia to the story. I added that I threw the ball so hard it gave me a hernia. I even went into detail about how I was carried off the field on a stretcher and taken to the hospital.

Never happened.

In my defense, I did have a hernia once. But I never had to go to the hospital. And then, being unable to help myself, one night onstage, I blurted out that on the way to the hospital my pecker turned black and was really swollen.

Never happened.

The worst was when I decided one night to put words into the catcher's mouth that he did not utter.

"You can really pitch, Mr. Jordan!"

To which I supposedly replied, "I can catch, too!"

Never happened.

Good Lord, what is wrong with me? I sometimes think I need to be watched after. The truth, especially in the case of this amazing story, is so much better without adding fictional devices to hold the audience's attention.

Years later, I was performing my show in Palm Springs, California. There was a rumor that Michelle Obama was going to come to see me and bring six of her girlfriends. They were all in Palm Springs having a "girls only" week. And that Sunday evening, sure enough, I glanced out at the audience and in the front row was Michelle Obama with six of her friends.

I was beyond honored. Thank goodness I had about forty years of performing under my belt, or I might have freaked out.

I mean, really.

Michelle Obama? In all her dignified glory.

For some reason, I knew the moment I saw her in the front row that the story needed to be told without any embellishment. There is something very direct and open about the way Mrs. Obama looks in your direction.

There is great beauty in knowing what you see is what you get, and I felt I owed her the same.

When the show was over and I met our former First

HOW Y'ALL DOING?

Lady, I was glad she'd heard the story of my last first pitch in its entirety without any added bells and whistles. She was very complimentary about the show and especially about that particular story. Her friend Valerie Jarrett also expressed pleasure at hearing the story of my last first pitch.

I have tried, over the years, to remember this valuable lesson. And I thought I was on my way to telling stories without embellishment. But then, one night, the gay boys in my audience were hooting and hollering louder than usual, and it happened.

I simply could not help myself.

"So, after I hurled that baseball with all my might, honey, I developed a hernia! They had to take me off the field on a stretcher. That hernia made my pecker turn black and blue . . ."

Oh well.

And on it goes.

UNTIL WE MEET AGAIN

***The happiest times of my life were spent
as a kid on vacation in Daytona Beach.***
Our family, with several other families from our church,
had a set summer ritual. Every June, we would load up
the station wagons and head to Florida. We always stayed
at the same place, the Aku Tiki Inn, and we always had
a room with a balcony overlooking the Atlantic Ocean.

It was heaven.

For me, the best part of the whole trip was the drive
down Interstate 75 to Florida. I suppose it was the year-
long anticipation of this vacation that made the drive so

special. It was all tied up with summer and all the expectations that come from sitting in a school desk all year long waiting with crazy anticipation for summer to begin. We would leave Chattanooga before daybreak and stop for an early lunch of Chick-fil-A sandwiches. Back then, Chick-fil-A was known as the Dwarf Grill but it really looked like a Dwarf House, which it was called years later, and its only location was in a suburb outside of Atlanta.

And it really was a dwarf house. It was a magical place that had tiny doors that led in and out of the restaurant, just for the kids.

After filling up on those delicious chicken sandwiches, we would pile back into our woody station wagons and hit the road. We would push down the backseats and lay a single mattress right on top for us kids. The windows were kept wide open as we hoped to catch a breeze. The heat in the Deep South is practically unbearable in the summertime. As my daddy drove, the twins and I would play all kinds of games and argue constantly about what section of the mattress belonged to whom.

I always wanted the section by the back window so I could have a view of the highway, vanishing as we drove forward. I was a dreamy child who loved to look out windows and ponder things. To watch things disappear into the early morning mist.

HOW Y'ALL DOING?

After our glorious week in Daytona Beach ended, we would pile back into the station wagon and head home. I, once again, fought for the view of the vanishing highway.

It was then I realized how hard goodbyes can be. Every year as we left Daytona, I was absolutely bereft. I did not want to leave the beach and go home. The year I was twelve, I even cried. Huge silent tears ran down my face as I theatrically smashed my head against the window, with my back to my family.

Something extraordinary had happened to me that summer and I never wanted to leave. I had developed a crush on a cute blond-headed boy. He was nut brown from being out in the sun and he had white hairs on his arms like baby duck down.

He was also a super athlete. He could do a half gainer off the diving board, and I thought he was coolest person I had ever met. Though he was slightly older than me, he took a liking to me and treated me like a little brother.

I know now that he was my first real crush. I had asked for his address so we could keep in touch. I treasured that piece of paper with his address on it and stared at his handwriting like a lovesick puppy dog. Even though it was fifty years ago, I've never forgotten where he lived. He told me he lived in Nashville, around Harding Place. Gosh, I remember it like it was yesterday. I remember how he made me feel and I remember simply dying inside on the way home, staring out at the lonely highway. Somehow, I knew I would never see the blond-haired boy again.

I was right.

When we arrived back home, I got my mother to help me compose a letter, telling him how much I enjoyed his company and how I hoped to hear back from him. We put a stamp on it and dropped it in the mailbox outside our house.

I put the flag up and hoped I would receive word soon.

But I never heard back.

As I finished the last story for this book, I felt the same way. I felt as if I were staring out the window, watching the scenery vanish, taking me farther and farther from the nut-brown, blond-haired boy who could do a half gainer off the diving board.

Writing can sometimes be a very lonely endeavor. You sit, lost in thought, pondering, trying to find the right words, with your mind as your only companion.

But the writing of these stories was different. It was a rather joyous thing, as I felt the presence of all my lovely new friends from Instagram with every word.

I did not want the experience to end.

And so it shan't. It shall not end. And I have no worries about hearing back as I did with the blond-haired boy, as

HOW Y'ALL DOING?

I know my followers will be with me as long as there is an Instagram or something similar.

I am a font of stories. I can launch into storytelling mode at a moment's notice. When friends say, "I have heard that story a million times and I never tire of hearing it," my heart is warmed.

So, to all my dear new friends, this is not goodbye forever. It is only goodbye for now. Goodbye till I get revved up and ready to launch into a whole bunch of new stories.

See you then.

ACKNOWLEDGMENTS

As with all my accomplishments in life, this book would not have been possible without the love and support of many people.

First and foremost, I need to thank "mama and the twins." When my daddy's plane went down in 1966, it was just us four. And it has remained thusly. We have weathered many storms and it has only brought us closer. They believed in me in times when I did not have enough sense to believe in myself.

I would also like to thank my best friend, Mike Lotus. He "cracked the whip" when necessary, as I can be a little undisciplined. He also reminded me of many stories I had told him over the years. Stories that I had completely forgotten about. He has a brilliant mind like a sieve. And was indispensable during the writing process.

This is my second book, but this is the first book I have written with the encouragement and wise oversight of Elle Keck, my editor and now friend. Her encouragement and light-but-effective touch guided me and kept me on our scheduled path. Most important, it was Elle's patience that drew me to her. At sixty-five years of age,

Acknowledgments

the idea of writing a book and battling the technology needed in this day and age scared me out of my wits. Elle took on all the challenges and kept me on course with her unwavering faith in the vision for my book.

I must not neglect to thank my "team" at BRS/Gage, David Shaul, Sarabeth Shedeen and Amy Abell-Rosenfield. They have worked so hard to keep me working and relevant, which is not easy in the ever-changing world of entertainment.

Finally, a deep bow to all my Instagram friends—for it was y'all who made this possible. You accepted me as your gay uncle, your "guncle," which inspired me during a difficult and uncertain time.

Enough with the acknowledgments, let's get back to talking about my favorite subject, ME!!!